BOWL. SLEEP. REPEAT.

BOWL. SLEEP. REPEAT.

INSIDE THE WORLD OF ENGLAND'S GREATEST-EVER BOWLER

Jimmy Anderson
with Felix White

An Hachette UK Company
www.hachette.co.uk

First published in Great Britain in 2019 by Cassell, an imprint of
Octopus Publishing Group Ltd
Carmelite House
50 Victoria Embankment
London EC4Y 0DZ
www.octopusbooks.co.uk

This edition published 2020

Distributed in the US by
Hachette Book Group
1290 Avenue of the Americas
4th and 5th Floors
New York, NY 10104

Distributed in Canada by
Canadian Manda Group
664 Annette St.
Toronto, Ontario, Canada M6S 2C8

ISBN 978-1-78840-169-2

A CIP catalogue record for this book is available from the British Library.

Printed and bound in the UK

10 9 8 7 6 5 4 3 2

Publishing Director: Trevor Davies
Senior Editor: Pollyanna Poulter
Art Director: Juliette Norsworthy
Production Controller: Grace O'Byrne
Copy Editor: Caroline Taggart
Proofreader: Abi Waters
Typesetter: Ed Pickford

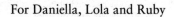
For Daniella, Lola and Ruby

Contents

Chapter 5, On Tour

Chapter 6, Knowing Me, Knowing You-y

Chapter 7, Ashes to Ashes

Chapter 8, And Another Thing...

Introduction

We set it, we bowl to it and we take the wickets.

They'd be lost without us.

A Bowler in a Batsman's World

It's not easy being a fast bowler. Some people might think it is, but it's not. The beauty of cricket, it is regularly observed, is that it allows every type of person to exist within it; all shapes and sizes put into a jigsaw puzzle of a team in a ceaseless tug-of-war with one another. I'd be prepared, in part, to agree. But it becomes problematic when you decide that your particular piece in the puzzle is going to be in the shape of the guy or girl who bowls fast.

Fast bowlers are the only people ever expected to do anything remotely close to physical exertion on a cricket pitch. There are batsmen who spend their time waiting for a ball to arrive. They wait. They watch. They occasionally hit. When not performing their prime purpose of duty, they prefer to spend their time in the field, having a chat, readjusting their caps, suddenly with all kinds of opinions and expertise on how to bowl. That or staring into middle distance in the dressing room trying to Jedi mind-trick their failings outside off stump from their DNA.

Wicketkeepers crouch, stand, catch. Mainly, though, they talk. They talk a lot. Many of them consider their most pertinent contribution to the game as having five days of stand-up material to keep everyone entertained and engaged, not least the viewers at home through the stump mics, rather than any kind of serious physical conditioning.

Even spinners don't know how easy they have it. They lollop up in a kind of laconic skip that you don't see anywhere else in life. If we are going to talk in real terms, it could never *really* be considered running; it could barely be considered exercise.

Then there's us.

When a fast bowler approaches the crease, he or she is essentially short-sprinting toward it. When we land, there is on average seven times our body weight going through our front foot. We are then expected to execute a complex minutiae of technical unravelling, before delivering the leather thing we're shuttling with us toward the batsman at the speed of a train. Then, whatever the consequences of that particular act, we have to do it again. Immediately. And again. And again. Test matches last five days. That's a lot of doing that. If we were at war in ancient times, we'd be the boulder carriers. But only if the boulder carriers were expected to be the generals, too. We're buying the tools, building the studio and making the record. We're writing the script, directing the film, making the tea and then putting someone else's name on the credits.

We put in so much effort that the laws of the game must be heavily weighted in our favour, I hear you ask?

That's where the injustice really starts to sting. Every single conceivable law in cricket is devised so that it suits the batsman. If there is any doubt, *any* doubt at all, the batsman will always receive the benefit.

Given that you're running so far, surely there's some leniency on where you land when you bowl, at least?

No. If you're a tenth of an inch over, you have to bowl the ball again, and all your work is not only considered void but actively punished, too. I've had wickets of world-class batsmen taken off me. World-class batsmen that you don't get second chances with because of it.

Well, surely, as a result, cricket has created an understanding environment in which fast bowlers are able to vent their frustration?

Nothing could be further from the truth. In fact, if you show any kind of 'dissent' toward an umpire or understandable anger toward a batsman, you are regularly fined slices of your match fee. I remember, for example, very lightly brushing a batsman's shoulder in a one-day international. I was fined. They said, 'The normally mild-mannered Anderson was solely to blame for the incident.' Even if I was, I think they could have spared me that. Another time, an umpire, who will remain nameless, got a decision totally wrong in an international. I think I might have very politely enquired how he could have made such an error of judgement. I was fined again.

It's not just at international level. I've experienced it since playing at clubs and school. I remember hitting someone on the pads in an under-17s game for Burnley. It was stone dead. I appealed. The umpire, to this day and to my total amazement, gave it not out. En route diligently back to my mark, I asked him why. 'I just didn't see it,' was his answer. I was being punished for the fact that either a) it was too fast or b) he wasn't looking. I should have known then that it was a sign of things to come. It's happened ever since. You ask out of genuine curiosity, 'Why wasn't that out?' I've had years of 'It's just not out, mate.' That's akin to answering a question with 'Because.'

OK, fine, but at least all fast bowlers will have each other's backs, then, even if they're on the other team?

Again, wrong. When you're facing an opposition fast bowler, if anything, they're likely to bowl quicker and will take greater satisfaction from hitting you as you brace for impact or duck for cover. It's lawless out there. Before helmets, there used to be a kind of unwritten fast bowlers' law. The tailender would borderline run for cover and the bowler would aim at the stumps. Job done. Nobody gets hurt. These days, with the evolution of protective gear, bringing more foolish bravery on our part with the bat, that sort of understood pact has gone out of the window. I was batting with Alastair Cook in the West Indies years ago. Cooky is potentially the greatest English batsman ever to have played the game. Fidel Edwards was running in and bowling 90-miles-an-hour rockets at me and 80-miles-an-hour dobblers at Cooky. There's no justice. I don't know why Fidel was prioritizing his efforts, but I was seething at the other end, thinking to myself, 'No wonder Cooky's unbeaten on a hundred for the umpteenth time.' He was dishing it up on a length to him and trying to knock me out. I can't win. Cooky, very admirably for a batsman, even acknowledged it and was trying to get me off strike, if purely out of guilt.

I've even had it with team-mates. Stuart Broad, whom I've spent over a decade bowling in tandem with for England, and whom I like to think of as an off-field friend and an on-field ally, did it to me very recently. I was pitched against him in a county game, Notts vs Lancs. We've rarely played against each other, having been the

England opening-ball partnership for so long. Without it being said, I felt it was a given that we'd both bowl full at each other, nothing short or dangerous, you know, what with life being hard enough for both of us as it is. He bowled me a handful of full balls and then one right at my throat, which I gloved to slip. I thought that was very interesting, that he felt the need to bounce me. I thought, right, next innings he's getting it. Fortunately for him, by the time he came out to bat, the ball was swinging, so I was pitching the ball up. He edged me to first slip. Of course, first slip dropped it. This is the life of a fast bowler, you show some mercy and that's the hand karma deals you. Stuart had the audacity to hit me for four through extra cover next ball. I saw red. I bounced him. I had to. There's only so much you can put up with. Anyway, he'd made his bed the innings before. Well, at least cricket has been going long enough and evolved into the modern world sufficiently that the gear has been developed to offer no distraction?

You're not going to believe this. But to this day, fast bowlers still cut a big hole into the front of their shoes. It's so that when we land, our feet aren't crushed inside the boot like a ballet-dancer's toes, folded backward. So, that's the help we get there. We're given nice new boots to wear and then we have to take to them with scissors like a manual labourer, so they don't cause us immense pain when we're doing the thing they're designed to help us with.

Take into account that, as I write this, I'm 36. I've been doing this a long time. That's nearly two decades of watching batsmen flay at balls that they should have left well alone, in situations where the shot beggars all belief, like being caught out cow corner when we are batting to save the game, then walk back into the dressing room and have the nerve to say, 'That's just the way I play.' They say it as if wielding some kind of artistic licence in a period drama. I've lost count of the number of times I've been lacing up my boots, muttering under my breath, when my rightly earned mid-innings sleep has been stolen from me because the batsmen have been bowled out on a pitch that has 'suddenly become unplayable'. Then the fast bowlers are left to run in again – did I fail to mention? – in searing heat, because cricket is only ever played in the summer, and save everyone all over again, like dogs with a deeply misplaced sense of loyalty.

England's long-time bowling coach, David Saker, would go mad with it. He'd come in after practice, venting, 'I'm sick of it. You see them coming in and they'll be saying, "The ball's seaming."' He'd be shaking his head wildly, turning incrementally deeper shades of red. 'The ball is rock-hard leather, with a rope on it that stands out. It's a grass wicket. Of course it's going to seam. That's the point of the game.' What I think David was trying to express was, what you'll learn is, that it's never a batsman's fault when they get out. It's 'the light was shining in my eyes, so I couldn't see', 'the sight screen is off centre' or, one of my personal favourites, 'I didn't expect him to bowl that.' If batsmen had it their way, the bowler would have to give a heads-up on where they are going to land the ball for them before each delivery.

I could pick out enough anecdotes to fuel a full book's worth on this subject alone, but to spare it becoming a tome of Morrisey proportions and tone, I'll leave it at this. In a particularly difficult test match recently, a batsman, who shall remain nameless, turned up on the morning of the third day and said, 'Phwoar, feels like day four or five, dunnit?' I'd bowled 40 overs because the batsmen had been skittled, collectively, all out in 30. Containing my disbelief, I asked, 'What do you mean?' He said, 'I'm shattered.' He'd only been actively involved in the game fleetingly, having got a ball that 'would have got out anyone' (that's what we tell batsmen sometimes to keep the peace and their deeply fragile egos at rest). This is what we, as bowlers, have to put up with. Not only a shouldering of responsibility, but a genuine lack of social tact, too. The batsmen always get the plaudits, they're always the captain, they're always considered the thinkers, the intelligent ones, the public-school boys. The more I've played, the more I've broken down the myth. It's like being woken from a lie. They like to say they are smart, because we do the hard yards, so it supposedly stands to reason. They'll stand there hoping the camera has caught their favoured profile, say, 'It's all up here' and point to their temples. The captain will take credit for the fields. It's the bowler who's setting them. We set it, we bowl to it and we take the wickets.

They'd be lost without us.

It's tough being a bowler in a batsman's world.

CHAPTER 1

A Peugeot With My Name on It

It was useful to come from

a town where sport was the

defining characteristic.

Burnley and Becker

Until I was 19, I had spent my entire life, bar very fleeting moments, in Burnley. For someone predisposed to throwing himself around as his sole source of entertainment, it was useful to come from a town where sport was the defining characteristic. The football ground, Turf Moor, became the team's home ground in 1883 and remains it to this day. They have a 'cricket stand end' that is located right next to where I played growing up. These days, they get 20,000 people into the ground every week. Burnley's population is under 80,000 in total. That's how much the town revolves around sport. Though famous for its cotton production in the 18th century, and with many being proud that it still provides a home for functioning medieval buildings, as far as I was concerned, growing up in Burnley was just a massive excuse for sport.

I was always outside as a kid. I used to play superheroes with my next-door neighbour. I'd be Spiderman and he was Batman. We would chase each other around the streets for hours, tagging each other and repeating. It never got boring, somehow. It was certainly never lacking in competitive edge. One day, he was in pursuit of me and, both taking the game as seriously as ever, especially as it was reaching its business end (it was nearly time for tea), I ran onto my porch to try to evade him. Our front door was open. I darted in, slammed it behind me and momentarily paused, considering myself the winner. A second later, he came flying through the panel at the bottom of the door. The glass shattered in his wake. I remember turning around to see him among the rubble, stretched out horizontally in true superhero style, and respecting his commitment to the cause. My mum wasn't as impressed, certainly not with me. Thankfully the glass pane was the only damage done.

My granddad was a wicketkeeper and a single-figure golfer, while my dad and his brothers were footballers and cricketers. They played to a decent standard, too. It meant that huge chunks of my early years were spent watching them from the touch line and then at half-time or tea, whatever it may be depending on the sport, emulating what I'd just seen with all the other kids. The life was handed down in that respect. The joys of it were stitched into my day-to-day. I'll always be grateful for that. I took the lead, and I ran with it, in a big way.

Of course, with all the life-affirming stuff, I inherited the competitiveness, too. My dad would never let me win at anything. He was like the dad in *The Fast Show*, smashing the ball past me at tennis and counting the score out loud, '40-0.' This applied to any sport – even board games – when we were trying to 'relax'; things like Trivial Pursuit or Monopoly. He was so competitive. It's not cryptic where I got my deep distaste for losing at anything. When I reached 15 or 16 and started occasionally to beat him at golf (owing mainly, in truth, to the handicap difference), we would come home and my mum would know which one of us had lost.

I would usually be in a filthy mood, but on notable occasions, if still infrequent, my dad would be the one looking gutted. She didn't need to ask. It was a subtle power shift, but I think that was actually pretty formative for me. I'd know, when I had beaten him, that I had done it on merit.

If you play a lot of sport, you generally lose a lot. Cricket can be quite an individual sport and if I have a bad game now, I'm brutally honest with myself in my own personal debrief. People tend to find excuses, especially at amateur or club level. It'll be, 'We lost the toss', 'The umpires were against us' and so on. But successful teams don't find excuses – they accept it and then fix it. That initiation really gave me the tools to deal with improvement and loss. I might have spent weekends sulking because I'd been bankrupted again at Monopoly while watching my dad build hotels on Fleet Street, but that helped me really. Losing is a part of sport, and it was certainly a crux of my growing up. It's about finding a way to deal with it. I've certainly had to, because I've lost a lot.

As I grew up, the activity might have evolved from chasing Batman across the streets, but I'd still be constantly running around, playing with my mates, using any excuse I could to be active. Even when there weren't others around, I'd be bowling, throwing a basketball, playing tennis or kicking a football against the wall at the side of the house. Any surface and any wall could be turned into some kind of gladiatorial arena for sporting glory. It required imagination, but I didn't ever let little details like there not being a goal, a hoop, stumps, a net or opponents get in my way. During the summer in particular, even for a family in love with sport, I would drive my parents to distraction. While Wimbledon was on, I'd turn the front room into an appropriation of a sports-bar-cum-tennis-court. I'd wake up, set the front room up and wait for the coverage to begin, armed with a racquet and a softball. The sofa was the net. As I watched, I'd try to recreate every shot I'd seen, re-enacting action replays almost in real time to the television coverage.

I daren't search for any kind of relevant link between them, but swiftly following my stint as Spiderman, the next superhero I aspired to be was Boris Becker. He was given a great deal of reverence on the television, which was always showing reruns of him winning the tournament at 17. I think the catalyst for my fixation, though, was more in the aesthetic. I loved the way he swayed as the ball was in the air, just before he served, but most pertinently I respected that he had managed to find a way to validate diving around as a profession. His diving volleys at the net were worshipped by everyone. It was a little light-bulb moment for me that someone could charge around, throw themselves into the air in front of lots of people and it not just be an acceptable form of employment, but a universally applauded and enviable one at that. That's all the prompting I was looking for. It became ingrained in everything I did. Stopping a cricket ball. Slide-tackling in football. Diving volley in tennis. I never perfected either of the last two, but Boris provided that immediate inspiration to play sport; at first just tennis, but then a more widespread dream of what a life in professional sport might mean. I think that's a special thing, to be able to inspire, so I'll always be grateful to him for communicating that from the tennis courts, through the television, into my front room in Burnley. It's potentially Boris-inspired, too that, later in life, I've often considered that if any other language was to suit my frequent mood, it would be German.

As a result of all this sporting input to the senses, school, or at least the academic side of it, was never at the forefront of my mind. Making sure I'd done my homework was a huge challenge for my parents. I look back with a lot of sympathy for them now – throughout the weekend they would be constantly nudging me to do it. I would ignore them till the last possible minute and usually get round to attempting it exhausted, covered in cuts and/or mud on a Sunday night. When I got to school itself, I'd sit at the back and populate my days with staring out of the window, in a football- or cricket-themed reverie. I really had the skill down of learning to nod and repeat teachers' phrases at the right times so that my daydreaming could slip by uninterrupted.

I don't think my parents were particularly concerned about this. They were really encouraging of everything that piqued my interest in general, but they did try to ensure that I was at least given the option to explore other things. I did English A level as a vague compromise in case I ever needed to do sports journalism. They once sent my sister and I to keyboard lessons together. It was immediately quite tangible to the teacher which one of us had the discipline required to be a musician. It wasn't me. I sat there watching my sister pick up scales as if a dormant muscle memory had just been awakened, while I twitched and irritably shifted around in my seat, wishing to be outside again. It was my one and only lesson. She's a Grade 8 pianist now and, to this day, at Christmas will play piano for everyone when we all congregate back in Burnley. I'd be lying if I said I didn't regret that, but I was too far gone by then. I think it was a relief to her to find something else, because she wasn't really into sport. She would humour me for a bit in the back garden, bowling underarm while I scratched around. I'd bowl at her, letting her hit some, then get bored with it, start doing it properly and get her out. I don't think she particularly enjoyed playing sport with me. She certainly didn't acknowledge or appreciate my thirst for wicket-taking the way others did later on.

Sport was quickly becoming the only thing that motivated me at all. If it was on television, any sport, anywhere, I'd be watching it. This included snooker on my grandparents' television. It was black and white. I was so hooked that I was very happy to watch snooker players pot grey balls all day, without considering that colour might be a useful visual aid to the game.

My local football team, Brierfield Celtic, took over Saturdays from when I was about eight-years-old. I played centre back like the other name on my genuine, slightly left-field, list of heroes; Burnley's very own Steve Davis. We wore black and red vertical stripes, like AC Milan. It's fair to say that we hadn't quite perfected the Italian sweeper system like our inspiration's trademark style, though, and my desperation to be involved in the game all the time left me a little lacking in Mr Davis's positional sense. I'm a bit like that now still with football – you could watch a whole game and need to ask me afterwards, 'What position were you playing?' I must have affected games in some kind of positive way, if for exuberant expression alone, because we went to France to play in a tournament that we did pretty well in. We got knocked out on penalties. I like to think that the experience braced me unknowingly for what a career playing for England might be like, even if it was in a different sport eventually.

I did try rugby, too. My dad didn't play it, so I wasn't predisposed to it, but a friend, noticing my endless appetite for running around, approached me like a scout.

'You might make a good winger, you know.'

'What's that?'

'Doesn't matter.'

He sold it to me that if I came and played, I could throw myself about and sprint around a field lot. I stopped him there, said, 'Say no more' and agreed to play the following Saturday. When I arrived, I began to worry about what I'd let myself in for. I was a bit hazy on the rules. It suddenly struck me that there was a substantial amount of physical danger to it. Watching boys infinitely wider and taller than me put in gum shields didn't fill me with confidence, either.

The game began and, starting to realize there might be some limits and conditions to my sporting endeavours after all, trying to stay out of the way as much as was realistically feasible, I was eventually passed the ball. People started shouting at me. There was no one in front of me. I could see the try line in the distance. '*Run.*' I set off. There was no one in my peripherals at first. I was thinking, 'Jesus. I'm going to do this. I'm going to score a try.' As I did, panicking for the line, the sound of a stampede grew louder and closer. The turf at the club was relatively, shall we say, inconsistent. There were craters everywhere, dips and divots in the pitch. I hit one. My legs buckled. I fell, clutching the ball in foetal position. I'd tackled myself. I lay there, alone, bracing for impact, thinking, 'Yeah, I'm not going to do this again.' I ended up on the bottom of a heap. *All* sport might not be for me. It was the only game of rugby I've ever played.

As well as going to France for football, it would be the destination with the family, too, if we were getting away. We would have an annual holiday there, all packed into the back of the car, which informed most of my earliest memories of listening to music. It'd be tapes of things like Blondie, Cyndi Lauper, David Bowie, Elvis Costello and Peter Gabriel. It was a decent initiation for the guitar-music burst of the mid-to-late 1990s. The northwest was totally consumed by that at the time. I loved Oasis, Blur, Cast, Dodgy, the Manics and the Stereophonics. That in turn was the inspiration to leaving Burnley for a night out on my own for the first time in my life. Me and a group of friends went to see James at the MEN Arena. It was a very big deal to all of us. Amid the high anticipation of the journey into town – on the infamous X43 bus, which was always akin to a ticket to Charlie's Chocolate Factory when I was young because it was the only known route into Manchester – my friend Nicola lost my ticket. I only had £12.50 and managed to blag another from a tout for the entirety of what was in my pocket. I really earned that first-ever gig. It was worth every penny. It also inspired a brief interest in becoming a bass player in a band. I tried it once. It wasn't my calling.

I was so fixated on sport that I didn't really drink until I was 14 or 15, which believe it or not was quite late compared to all my friends in Burnley. Ironically, when I got to 18, the social aspect of cricket led to a little bit more of that world. I'd play a game on Saturday and end up in town at a club that evening. When I was growing up, if you were up past midnight, the only place to be, literally, was Panama Joe's. It had the stickiest of sticky floors and a big wooden dance floor in the middle. It was the only place that was open, and we were perfectly happy with our lot. On Thursday nights, after cricket practice, it was 10p-a-pint night. Ten pence. A pint. I think the drinks were fairly watered down. You got a plastic neon glow in the dark pint pot, which you'd keep taking back to the bar. 10p refills. I'd go out with a tenner, drink all night, get a taxi home and come back with change. We loved it and, in such a community-orientated world, Panamas was the one place that you could absolutely be assured of not bumping into your parents. Apart from one night when a mate forgot that he was supposed to get home for one in the morning. At two, an hour after curfew, we were all getting toward the pound mark in our night's expenditure and word was going around the club that a parent was wandering around in his coat and slippers looking for his son. We were all shimmying around the corners of the dance floor using other people as shields in case it was ours. Thankfully it wasn't my dad. My mate got dragged home that night. The building is still there, but it's definitely not called Panama Joe's any more.

I used to love a Saturday afternoon on Turf Moor with the whole family watching Burnley. We had a season ticket for a number of years and most of my family still do. I look back with such fondness on those days out. I can still see my granddad shouting at the ref and taste the half-time Bovril. I idolized the players: they're the first autographs I ever got, waiting for the team during warm-ups. One of my earliest memories of genuine devastation was not being allowed to go to the Sherpa Van Trophy in 1988 at Wembley. I was six. Fortunately, we've had a few trips to Wembley since, which are really cherished memories. We'd make the odd away day. Most memorably we went away to Huddersfield, which was terraced at the time. I snuck through to the front, so I could watch right by the pitch. John Deary scored in front of me. He ran toward the away end. I stuck out my hand and he gave me a lusty high five. It was the highlight of my life at that point. I couldn't believe it. John Deary! I didn't wash my hand for a week.

Cricket, though, had begun to capture my imagination beyond just the playing itself. I had run round to my friend's house to watch the World Cup final in 1992: he had Sky. I was desperate for England to win, but felt a strange fascination piqued by Wasim Akram. He was bowling swing that felt as if it cast a spell over people. With consecutive balls he got Alan Lamb and Chris Lewis, both of whom stared back at him for a split second as if seeking an explanation of how the ball had just done what it had. I wanted to *play* for England, but in that moment, I wanted to *be* Wasim Akram. The different inflections of the game across the world began to open those places up to me. I'd listen to Tony Cozier on the commentary in the Caribbean while England toured there and with my mind I'd be painting exactly what was going on and what was happening. All those characters really sold the game to me. It was an appeal that cricket alone had.

I was always James. My family call me James, my children call me James, my wife calls me James, all her friends call me James. Jimmy was an invention through cricket. It began in the cricket club, where everyone tends to find nicknames for each other, and it stuck. I don't think my mum ever took into account, when choosing the name, that there would be all the possible variations of it. She's never really liked Jimmy. She hates it when the announcer at a cricket ground calls me 'Jimmy Anderson from the Vauxhall End'. Unfortunately for her, more often than not these days, that's what they'll say. I was up for BBC Sports Personality of the Year in 2018 and they asked whether I wanted to be called James or Jimmy. They said, 'We would suggest you go with Jimmy, because that's what everyone knows you as.' I had to take my mum to one side and explain that I was really sorry, but it was going to have to be Jimmy tonight. She's come to accept it. I was relieved, for her more than anything, when they chose to call the end at Old Trafford – which is to this day a very surreal honour – the 'James Anderson End', rather than Jimmy. At least she got that one. Whenever I meet anyone now, I introduce myself as Jimmy. I don't really mind. I've been called a lot worse.

Most of the people I met in Burnley then have remained close friends. There were twin girls that we knew because our dads played together, and we grew up going round listening to music, then drinking Smirnoff Ice and so on. It was like that with lots of people. The cricket club forged such community. There would be all kinds of age groups all in the same place, all day. It's only now that I realize what a blessing that was. It's quite rare to come across that these days, and sport, or cricket in this case, really did provide it. There were so many tools for life that you'd pick up without even knowing it. I was shaped, really, by the people at that club. I owe it a lot.

I was in awe of my Burnley team-mates who represented Lancashire, too. That seemed a long way away to me when I was playing there in my mid-teens. Mark Harvey grew up at Burnley and went on to play professionally for Lancashire. He was held in high regard by all the kids at Burnley – a local celebrity, if you will. He would often come back down to the club in his sponsored Peugeot 206. His name was printed on the side. We couldn't believe that someone from Burnley was playing for Lancashire and had a car with his name on it. It felt like a bit of an implausible dream, but it was something to aim for. Having a Peugeot with my name on it. I'd have taken that then with both hands. I didn't ever think that I'd be able to forge a career in any of the sports I played, but I hoped and prayed. After all, I didn't really stand out at any.

CHAPTER 2

Well, That's a First

We celebrated and, as that calmed down, someone turned to me as we were huddled around and said, 'Isn't that a hat trick?'

Oh. Wait. Yeah, I think it is.

All the Gear

In club cricket, especially when you're starting out, you do a lot of borrowing gear. At every club at every level of every age group across the country, somewhere at the bottom of a locker there's a club kit bag with cobbled together versions of bits of different kit. You have to dig through it manically to assemble any kind of passable cricket gear. These bags have all got the same smell. They're a petri dish for mud, grass and sweat, but sort of left to fester in a non-specific experiment for years; a hotch-potch of disused pieces of lost property from the ages.

They're memorabilia archives of unloved and forgotten equipment. None of it ever matches. You'll be hard pushed to find a right-hand glove that matches a left hand, for example. You'll be walking out to bat with two left-handed pads and a thigh guard round your chest.

I remember having to bat as a kid and wincing as I put everything back on that had just been sweated through by whoever had batted last. The box was the most dubious. Who shares a box? I never understood that. If you're a batsman, the first thing you'd bring would be your own box, right? Some of them never learn. Alastair Cook, in his last ever test innings, one of the most anticipated and emotionally loaded knocks you'll ever see, lost his just before. I had to lend him mine. This man was playing his 161st test match. I didn't pass it down like Excalibur, presenting it to him on one knee and saying, 'You must wear it well', as some kind of symbolic passing of the guard. I was more seething that, after all these years, I was still sharing gear with forgetful batsmen.

When I did get to the stage where my parents were prepared to buy me some of my own gear, not only was it a huge relief, but it was a big decision.

Who do I identify with?

Who am I?

It wasn't about any sense of practicality per se – it was more a projection of my intended self. If I dress the part, I'll be the part, I thought. That wasn't exclusive to me. It was endemic. A lot of kids had obviously done some thinking and some watching of television. Graham Thorpe had a big summer batting wearing a headband under his helmet. Suddenly that was a prerequisite for batting in Burnley. There'd be 12-year-olds going out to bat with a headband underneath a helmet which, given the size of everything, often made them look less like the dogged and masterful manipulator of field settings Graham Thorpe, and more as if they were wearing two hats. Those who modelled themselves more on Alec Stewart would suddenly turn up for the new season in sweatbands, too. They'd look at you, needlessly defensive, like 'What you looking at? I've always worn these. This is who I am', while twirling their bat and readjusting their pads (Stewart's pre-delivery routine).

Already identifying myself, by default more than anything, as a bowler, it was a little harder for me to project my intended self through gear. There was much less of it, obviously. I began with the aesthetics. On the television I had seen Dominic Cork and Darren Gough run in at an angle. So I would run in at a wholly unrealistic and exaggerated angle, just on the assumption that would make me the player they were. There was one thing I could use, though, to be a bowler. Bowling boots.

You couldn't be a bowler if you didn't wear bowling boots.

That's what everyone would think. It was distinguishing between one and the other. I'd think to myself, 'Right, I've got my bowling boots on, now I've got bowling head on.' To be fair, that is probably still what my mindset is now. It's dressing up for service.

My first proper pair of bowling boots were Duncan Fearnley. They were typical of bowling boots at the time, with a high ankle a bit like a basketball shoe. Obviously ankles take a bit of stress when you're bowling, so the theory was that this design would help with that. No one wears them anymore. Bowling boots are all a lot lower now. They did last me two whole seasons, though. There was something about having real bowling boots that made you feel like a real bowler.

If I was batting, I'd never wear the boots. That was a big no-no for me. As far as I was concerned, if you batted in your bowling boots, then you couldn't bat. It was effectively like walking out waving a white flag. Chris Martin from New Zealand, though a very gifted and successful bowler, was famed for maybe being the worst batsman of all time. Going in at number 11, he had so little confidence that he would bat in his bowling boots. Then when he was out and the innings was over, all he needed to do was take his pads and gloves off and he was ready to bowl. It was out of practicality – there was no point changing his shoes. He knew when he put his pads on that they were only going to be on for the amount of time it took to walk out to the middle, face a ball, then spin 180 degrees and walk immediately back.

As the nets developed at Burnley, too, and I got older, people used to take their own ball to nets. I bought one and sat at home on summer holidays, in the front room, doing my usual residency watching Wimbledon, and got the furniture polish out. I'd polish and polish and polish until I could see my face in it, like a fish-eye-lens Beastie Boys photo shoot on one side of the ball. I'd be roughing up the other side, thinking to myself like an evil genius, 'This is going to be unplayable when I get into the nets, mwahahaha.' In truth, I don't think it had any actual effect.

But that was me. A proper bowler with proper bowling boots and an incredibly shiny, highly doctored cricket ball. Ready for action.

I hadn't totally given up the ghost on batting at this stage. In fact, I think a part of me believed that once I got my first actual bat, all the stars would align. It was a Slazenger V100. I was maybe 12-years-old. It's still my favourite bat ever. I loved the stickers. It was the same as Neil Fairbrother used, one of my favourite Lancashire players at that time. It was very precious. At the end of the season I'd sand the bat, oil it and then leave it in the garage for the winter until indoor nets started, so it was nice and soft. I wouldn't like to lend it. You were mad if you lent your V100 out. People started getting their own bats and those who didn't would become quite Machiavellian. You'd get a guy walk out to bat without a bat in his hand and ask for the outgoing batsman's bat, backing him into a corner to lend it, just because they knew he had a nice new one. There was a lot of that.

I'd drive everyone mad knocking my V100 in. I'd do the edges, making sure it was smooth. There were all kinds of techniques – the hammer and ball that you could get from the cricket shop – but I decided the ball in a sock would be just as effective.

My family weren't happy with me that fortnight.

Everywhere I went I was carrying the new bat around, hammering it in with my ball in a sock. It sounded as if there was unexpected building work happening down the road.

Another trick, in moulding yourself to be the cricketer you wanted to be, was sanding the bat. It was like a very early form of social media – presenting to the world the person you wanted to be rather than the one you were. I used to go and net, edge the ball all over the place – there'd be balls flying off the toe end and off the shoulder – and learn to immediately sand the cherries off. I didn't want those marks on my bat. They were parts of my past to be air-brushed out with immediate effect. I'd leave the ones in the middle, though. When I'd walk out to the middle during a match, I'd see people going, 'Woah, he's good, look at that, he's never missed the centre of the bat.' Then they'd pause among themselves, scratching their heads and thinking, 'Why's he batting eleven, then?' Professional cricketers still do that now.

Firsts

Acquiring all my own gear for the first time not only felt like the beginning, but the pinnacle, too. Over the following pages are some other firsts that were to follow, some more successful than others.

First Ball as a Professional

Lancashire 2nd XI vs Surrey 2nd XI at Stanley Park, Blackpool, 2000
J M Anderson 16-4-72-0

My first delivery as a pro might be the worst ball I've ever bowled. I was playing for Lancashire 2nd XI at Blackpool CC, a place I'd played a few times before. Even though I was familiar with the ground and I'd played a number of times for the seconds as an amateur, I was still pretty nervous. I had begun to dread bowling, but inevitably got handed the ball. I started to run in. My legs felt a bit jelly-like and I lost concentration. I'm not sure exactly what happened next – I think my brain has banished it from my memory out of necessity – but I ended up jumping at the crease. I'd never jumped at the crease before. My back foot took out middle and leg stump at the non-striker's end and I ended up flat out on the deck. The umpire, Ian 'Gunner' Gould, who is now one of the best international umpires around, had his head in his hands. He just looked at me splayed out over the floor and said, 'What the hell was that, son?' That was my introduction to professional cricket.

First Wicket in First-Class Cricket

I J Ward c W K Hegg b J M Anderson

Lancashire vs Surrey at Old Trafford, 2002

19-4-65-2

It was a few games into the season. I had been playing in the second team and wasn't necessarily earmarked to play first-team cricket but, as ever, circumstances conspired to hand me an opportunity. Neil Fairbrother, my Slazenger V100 inspiration and general legend of the game, was still a Lancashire regular and feeling his way back from injury with a game in the 2nd XI. I ended up in the team with him and I took eight wickets. The story goes that he got on the phone straight away to the coach and said, 'You have to get him in.' I have always been a bit lucky like that. When you are making your way through the game, you don't just have to perform well, you also have to have the fortune to perform well in front of the right person at the right time. It was the same as my mate's mum who had seen me bowl years before and recommended me to Lancashire. Except this time it was England's Neil Fairbrother.

So, I was drafted in at Old Trafford for Lancashire First team.

We were playing the famous Surrey side that was packed full of serious batsmen, back-to-back internationals. I can still reel off the batting order. Mark Butcher, Ali Brown, Mark Ramprakash, Alec Stewart, Graham Thorpe, Adam Hollioake. It was pretty close to being the England team at that time. Good luck bowling them out. It was an intimidating baptism, because I knew every single player really well, from television more than anything. They were like celebrities to me.

Old Trafford had fast and bouncy pitches that were known to be conducive to reverse swing. True to form, it reversed a bit that day. I got one to reverse across Ian Ward who, before his presenting days, was a seriously good player and an England international, too. He nicked it to Warren Hegg. In the same game I got Mark Ramprakash out LBW. In retrospect, they were great players to bowl at as a first-class cricket birth. I had nothing to lose. If you can get any of those players out, even a couple of them, you are suddenly armed with the belief that you are capable of getting anyone in the world out. It doesn't make you invincible and it certainly doesn't mean you'll be able to do it automatically or with any regularity, but it's a necessary part of the progression. If I was having a rough time, I could always fall back on that memory and know that it wasn't beyond me to find a solution. I won't say I felt like I belonged immediately, but it did wonders for me in terms of my confidence.

First Wicket in International Cricket

A C Gilchrist b J M Anderson 124

England vs Australia at MCG, 2002

6-0-46-1

I don't remember a lot of landmarks. I have terrible memory for things like that. It's awful because people are always asking me how it felt to go past this record and that. Usually I just shrug and say, 'Yeah, it was all right', mainly because I don't have enough of a recollection of it to say any more. There's a lot of adrenaline, so maybe it would be optimistic to hope to be able to relive it in real time, too. I will always have total recall of my international debut, though, mainly because I was so nervous. It was a one-day game against the all-conquering Australia side of the 1990s. I was drafted in, as per, as a very last-minute scrabbling amid a lot of injuries. If I'm honest, when I got called into the squad, really out of practicality because I'd been with the Academy in Australia at the time, I didn't think I'd get to play at all. I was quite low down the pecking order and kept out there just in case of injuries. I'd watched the first game in Sydney and then, to my surprise as much as anyone else's, Nasser Hussein (during his reign as captain) came up during practice the day before the second one-dayer in Melbourne and said, 'You're playing.' I had to double check I'd heard him properly.

A debut at the MCG, then.

It was so last-resort that the kit I was wearing was massive for me.

It was a 'big fit' in general, they said. I looked like Tom Hanks in *Big* when he got shrunk. My fast-tracking into the side was such that there was no name or number on the back, either. The Australian fans were famously generous with their opinions, especially then, when they were winning all the time, and I knew I was going to get it. The MCG was under renovation, they'd knocked a quarter of it down, so there was an area of the ground that was only overlooked by construction work. I was waiting for Nasser to point to where everyone was fielding. I had everything crossed that he'd point to the safe zone I'd eyed in front of the building site.

He didn't.

There's an area at the MCG called Bay 13. It's basically where everyone congregates if they want to shout something at an Englishman, a safe zone for Pom-bashing. It's famous for being the place you're going to receive your abuse from. Nasser sent me there. Cheers. I was getting a lot of 'Water boy!' or 'Who the heck are you?' Obviously I couldn't point to my shirt to tell them; there was no name or number on it. I don't think they were asking particularly inquisitively anyway. Luckily we bowled first. If we'd been fielding second on a day-night game I dread to think what they'd have been like once they'd had a few drinks.

Not only did I not have a name, number or kit that fit, I didn't have an England helmet either. When I went out to bat with Craig White, I had to go out wearing the fielding helmet. This has an extra bar on the front that protects the chin, like a hockey goalkeeper. I felt a bit of an idiot batting in that. It looked as if I'd required or requested one more bar of protection than everybody else. I thought the 'closing your eyes, reaching into the kit bag and hoping for the best' days would be behind me if I played for England. It turns out not.

We bowled first. I remember being really, very seriously nervous. The opening batsmen were Adam Gilchrist and Matthew Hayden. I'd seen a lot of them on television and knew how destructive they could be, so when I look back now I think that I had good reason to be intimidated. Adam Gilchrist was one of the real revolutionaries of one-day cricket. It is common now to see short-form cricketers go hard at the ball from the off, with scoring rates of well over a run a ball. Gilly was pretty much the godfather for the whole movement. He kept wicket and batted seven in test matches, but he was so destructive in short-form cricket that he opened. That was unfortunate for me on my debut, because I opened the bowling. As with my first-class experience, my welcome into the international fold was against the best there was, maybe even ever.

My first overs went everywhere. I think I went for eight an over, which if it sounds like a lot now was even more then. When I returned for a second spell, with the field spread and Australia putting us to the sword in a way that I was so used to watching but not actually being a part of, I bowled Gilly a wide half volley. He was way past his century by then. His eyes just lit up. He tried, as they say, to hit the cover off the ball. It was slightly misjudged, maybe in disbelief that he'd got a ball like that in an international, and he got an inside edge onto the stumps. There was a sort of stunned silence around the G. It wasn't a comprehensively beaten bowled, a classic nick one off or a shouldering-arms leave LBW, but I could wait for those. A wicket is a wicket, and I was up and running. It calmed something in me. I remember thinking, 'I'm 20 years old, playing for England, it's a dream come true. It might only be one game, but I'll enjoy it while I'm here.'

We lost that game quite comfortably.

First Wicket in Test Cricket

M A Vermeulen b J M Anderson 1

England vs Zimbabwe at Lord's 2003

16-4-73-5

I'd played one first-class game at Lord's at the end of the previous year, but obviously it is the most daunting place imaginable to make a test debut. The place is so steeped in cricketing history that you do genuinely feel it everywhere. There's a hum that is very specific to it. It comes with its own bespoke working hazards, too, like having to watch out for Champagne corks popping and hitting you on the outfield. You didn't get that in Burnley.

I made my debut alongside Yorkshire captain Anthony McGrath. So there was a bit of a Roses rivalry present even there. David Graveney, the chairman of selectors at the time, gave us our caps on the boundary edge in front of the pavilion. There's a culture now, which I like, of ex-players giving speeches and handing caps to players they might have had a hand in helping on their way, but this was before then. Maybe it was impractical at the time because so many people were getting picked, in a kind of clutching at straws for the right formula.

I was just keeping my head down in general. It was quite surreal, so I decided, 'I'll not speak unless spoken to, I'll blend into the background as much as I can, until we're playing.' That was difficult, given that my hair was highlighted with blonde tints at the time. That's not a great way to not attract attention, to be honest. Maybe it's part of being young. I certainly got a few looks walking through the members' bit, studs echoing across what feels like a marble floor, as I went out to field with my dyed hair.

I felt totally numb. I wasn't really in tune with my body, if that makes sense. I suddenly felt alien in it. I was relying on all the muscle memory I had just to run in with the ball. That's all I had, run in on auto-pilot, begin running in with the ball and pray that it would get down the other end. I was just there, numbed out, letting Nasser set the field, telling myself not to do the weird jump and knock the stumps over in my wake as I had on my professional debut. I was aware there'd be a lot more people than Ian 'Gunner' Gould sighing at me if I did that again. Nasser decided that I didn't need a fine leg. My first over went for 17 runs. I kept getting clipped down there to the vacated area behind the wicketkeeper. I began to worry a bit: 17 off your first test over really doesn't read very well. To his eternal credit, Nasser ran up to me afterwards, put his arm round me and said, 'Sorry, that was my fault. Start again next over.' I've always had a fine leg from that point on.

There were times that season playing for Lancashire when Warren Hegg would say, 'Look, mate, don't worry about swinging it, just try and bowl as fast as you can.' At that point, I relied on the senior players to get me through with game plans and so on. A similar thing happened with England. The ball wasn't swinging much to begin with, so I reverted to my first form of wicket-taking, trying to bowl fast. Believe it or not, I think I beat Mark Vermeulen for pace. I don't say that much anymore. He was slightly late on it and it hit the top of middle and off.

It started swinging after that. I'd bowled Vermeulen from the Nursery End, but when it was swinging a bit more I bowled from the Pavilion End. I think it was just a natural thing to do but, ever since then, that has been the end I like to bowl from more regularly at Lord's. I ended up taking five wickets. On debut at Lord's. It's funny, because I've always felt as if my in-swinger, which becomes an out-swinger to the left-hander, has taken years to get right, or at least be comfortable with. Looking back at the wickets I took that day, though, I bowled it as well as I've ever done. Especially the ball to the left-hander Andy Blignaut. He nicked it to Mark Butcher at second slip. I probably didn't bowl it as regularly as I could have, in truth.

It was actually quite an enjoyable game in the end.

First Hat Trick

First Class County Championship, Lancashire vs Essex at Old Trafford, 2003

D D J Robinson c A J Swann b J M Anderson 11

W I Jefferson c W K Hegg b J M Anderson 19

N Hussain lbw J M Anderson 0

15-1-67-4

One Day International, England vs Pakistan at the Oval, 2003

A Razzaq c M E Trescothick b J M Anderson 17

S Akhtar c C M W Read b J M Anderson 0

M Sami b J M Anderson 0

9-2-27-4

I'd seen hat tricks before in the championship. After the second wicket, everyone in the field, regardless of the game situation, suddenly surrounds the bat and a game-within-a-game develops of trying to achieve this milestone for the bowler. I liked that because it felt as if, in a game where, as I've made clear, the odds are so indefinitely stacked against us bowlers, it afforded us a rare moment of complete support; small compensation. I remember watching Dominic Cork's hat trick against the West Indies at home on the telly: him appealing with arms stretched out, sun block across his face like war paint, and then being mobbed by everyone as the country celebrated.

That's how I'd imagined mine.

Instead, my first professional hat trick was a comparative gigantic anticlimax. We were playing Essex. The two openers looked as if they were struggling a bit to see the ball and I'd got them both with quite full and straight balls. My England captain, Nasser again, came to the crease just as the over ended. When it was my turn to bowl again, I'd forgotten about those two consecutive wickets. I'd logged the previous two dismissals and thought I'd bowl really full, right in the block hole at him. It hit him right on the foot, plumb in front. Given. We celebrated and, as that calmed down, someone turned to me as we were huddled around and said, 'Isn't that a hat trick?'

Oh. Wait. Yeah, I think it is.

The moment was gone.

I felt like recalling Nasser as he visibly hobbled off the pitch, to tell him. It took an age for him to disappear into the distance. The Essex players told me that when he eventually got into the dressing room, he chuntered, 'Why can't he do that when I bloody well ask him to?' That was very typical of Nasser.

I'd begun to grow a reputation of being able to bowl 'spells' of taking wickets without being consistent enough, which I was desperate to change. The hat tricks were an example of that. I managed to find rhythm and metronomic ability as my career went on, but these little moments, if frustrating that I couldn't always maintain them, acted as flags to everyone else – and for that matter to me too – of what might be possible.

I took another hat trick that year, in a one-day international against Pakistan at the Oval. Abdul Razzaq hit one down Marcus

Trescothick's throat; Shoaib Akhtar nicked one to Chris Read behind the stumps, one that I'd taken a bit of pace off, knowing he'd expect the opposite; then I bowled Mohammad Sami. Again, totally unbeknown to me, it made me the first ever Englishman to take a hat trick in one-day cricket.

I'd been hit around the ground at Old Trafford earlier in the series.

I was beginning to learn how bipolar the highs and lows of international cricket could be.

First (Golden) Duck

J M Anderson b D A Altree 0

Lancashire vs Warwickshire 2nd XI at Bulls Head Ground, Coventry, 2000

My first memory of getting a golden duck is in a 2nd XI match against Warwickshire. I came to the crease and the bowler was left-arm over. When you go out to bat, occasionally you'll ask, 'Is he doing anything?' Your partner at the other end can be varying degrees of helpful. At club or even 2nd XI level it'll be, 'Yeah, it's boomeranging...I think', without any specified direction, or 'I've got no idea what he's doing with the ball, but it's working.' The info I got from my batting partner on this occasion was genuinely useful: the bowler was swinging the ball consistently away from me. I thanked him and duly premeditated my opening shot as I scratched out my guard. Given the conditions I had just been alerted to, I shouldered arms to my first delivery. The safest option to the out-swinging ball, especially when you identify it pitching outside the line of off stump. The ball swung back *in* and cleaned up my middle and off stump.

I glanced straight over to the other batter. He greeted my glance with a shrug. That was my first golden duck.

Unfortunately, it would be far from my last.

First Time I Was Hit for Six

Club game, Burnley. No record. Best forgotten.

Being hit for six is a chastening experience. There's something psychologically quite scarring in the fact the ball can be safely in your hand, then, within seconds, over a stand or in the car park or in the trees. I've been hit into all of those directions.

It started happening a lot when I was 15 or 16 and playing for Burnley. You'd occasionally play against men, which is a seriously formative experience in itself, especially when they wouldn't ever dial down their competitive edge because they were playing against kids. But you'd also be facing boys who had suddenly become bigger, upward and outward, towering over others they'd been the same height as last year. I remember taking a wicket and having my, believe it or not, gleeful celebration cut short just at the sight of the incoming batsman. He was taller, and wider, than most my age. You know, the type that considers the technical rule number one of batting to be have your head looking directly up toward the sky at point of contact, front foot planted somewhere non-specific off to the leg side. That's how he hit me. It was a huge one.

Trying to bowl fast, I found this would happen a reasonable amount. People would swing wildly and, if they made any type of contact, the ball would disappear. The overseas pros in particular would often be quick onto a bouncer and hook it into the stands. I don't remember being too bothered by it, though. I was a wicket-taker, that was always what was tantamount to me, and I used to think, 'If the ball's going in the air, then there's a chance it will be caught.'

The biggest six I have been hit for was at Lord's in a one-day international. Abdul Razzaq, a victim to that first ever English limited-over hat trick years previously, was at the crease toward the end of the Pakistani innings, swinging at everything. When he was on form, he was the kind of person you didn't want swinging at everything, because he was such a clean hitter. He hit me straight down the ground on the on side, onto the top of the Mound Stand. I remember watching with an open mouth as the ball seemed to keep going and going. That's the thing with cricket – there's always a chance for revenge. It felt like it was hit a similar distance – if with slightly better technique – to my first experience of being struck for a maximum.

I have never been someone who could clear the ropes with ease myself. My first six came at Centurion Park in South Africa. When I say first six, this wasn't my first test-match six. This was my first six anywhere, at any level. That's how rare they are. Paul Harris, a left-arm spinner, was bowling and I was batting with Graeme Swann. Swanny was encouraging me to play some shots. I'm not sure to this day if he was winding me up or not. I played a slog sweep against Harris. I *was* trying to hit it hard, granted, but my intended and hopeful route was for four through mid-wicket. To my eternal surprise it flew off my bat, into the air and sailed over the rope! I couldn't believe it. I had a huge grin on my face for days after. Since then, my six-hitting has gone from strength to strength. I've now amassed four sixes in my career.

First Time Being Hit by a Bouncer

Dale Steyn
England vs South Africa at Headingley, 2008

Being the last of a dying breed of genuine tail-enders, with nowhere near the skill or reactions of the top order, I find that facing bouncers is unfortunately a daily occurrence. It's comparable to how, if you're scared of or allergic to a dog, it will somehow get a sixth sense and be more inclined to follow you around and jump on you. I've been hit a few times. One of the worst was by the West Indian Fidel Edwards, but the first was Dale Steyn. He hit me on the jaw. Fast bowlers' union my a**e. Obviously the helmet bears a huge brunt of the impact these days, which in part is unfortunate because it's made bowlers less self-conscious about bowling at head height. In Dale's case, the helmet did its job and absorbed the blow, but still left me with a big bruise on my jaw. There's always this surreal moment where it's as if time is momentarily suspended, you realize the ball is going to hit you on the head and there's nothing you can do about it. You brace for impact in that split second. The only thing I can liken it to is at school when someone hits you in the head when you're not expecting it and a bit harder than they were expecting to. It's a sucker punch. You have a tiny moment of not being sure if you should be angry or upset or whether you're seriously hurt or not. Fortunately, I've come out of most of my blows, if a bit shaken, totally unharmed.

First Time Run Out

J M Anderson run out (R Jadeja) 2

England vs India at Lord's, 2014

It is a genuinely common recurring nightmare for cricketers to dream of being run out. You're going for a single and trying to run, but you're running through treacle, or your pads are too big, or the other end seems miles away. No matter how hard you run, it gets further away. It's not too far from how it feels in real life sometimes. Getting run out is that nauseating feeling right in the middle of the Venn diagram between humiliating and traumatic. There are not many worse feelings in cricket.

I got run out at Lord's in a test match in 2014. In my defence, we were never winning the game. I think I was trying to get off strike: I hit it straight to Ravindra Jadeja, who I'd had a bit of back-and-forth with all series, and he ran me out. I ended up on my knees trying to get back, diving for my ground. Cricket writes those stories for you sometimes, and there's not much you can do about it. We'd collapsed, losing six wickets for 50 runs. I did feel a real sense of injustice, picking myself up covered in mud and waiting to shake hands with a jubilant Indian side, that I should be the one left on his knees to take the final hit when all the batsmen before me had got themselves out. Invariably being the last wicket to fall to lose a game, I've quite often borne the brunt of being out there when we lose. We were playing Australia in a world-cup game, for example, in 2015. James Taylor had anchored the innings to get us through our allotted overs. He was 99 not out when I joined him, at the non-striker's end. He got hit on the pads. They appealed. It was given out. We'd already set off for a run. I heard the cheers and instinctively stopped running. They threw the ball at the stumps, while I was stood there assuming it to be the end of the phase. James reviewed it and they gave it not out. I was then given out 'run out' because I had been short of my ground. James was left stranded on 99. It should have been a dead ball.

First Catch Dropped

Burnley CC vs Burnley FC, 1997
Burnley FC win by 3 wickets

One of the most humiliating moments I've had on a cricket field is when I've dropped a catch. It's probably worse than being run out. In part it's because I've always worked hard on my fielding and usually have a fairly safe pair of hands. The earliest one I remember was as a 15-year-old playing for Burnley CC vs Burnley FC. I was playing against some of my footballing heroes and that added a strange kind of pressure, even though they weren't cricketers. The football club needed four to win and the ball was hit high toward me at long on. It was one of those horrible ones that feels like it's up there for a very long time, giving you the time to change your mind three times about how you're going to catch it. Nerves struck and I closed my hands too keenly. The ball landed on my thumb and went over the boundary for six. In the humiliation of it all, I decided not to tell everyone that I was actually in quite a lot of pain. I found out later I'd broken my thumb.

On the other hand, it's a regular occurrence having people drop catches off my bowling. I try to blank it out of my mind. I think it's probably clear how I feel about it at the time.

The thing about cricket is, there's always another first around the corner, even if you've been playing for the best part of two decades. I'd say I've seen it all, but I probably haven't yet...

CHAPTER 3

The Art of Swing Bowling

With most of the best bowlers in the
world, they're not always technically that
'good', they just...bowl

Forever a Work in Progress

I know it sounds strange, but sometimes when I hear 'Jimmy Anderson has broken this record', or I see myself on TV, it feels like it's not actually me. I know that it is, but it can be too surreal to totally absorb. It's almost as if they're talking about someone else. Maybe in part it's because when I was growing up, I was really average. I'm not saying that to be modest, either. I was. As my best mate very kindly told the *Times* recently, I had a 'nice action, but he was just a decent club bowler.' Thanks, pal. It was true, though. It was all football, football, football at my school and when I used to play cricket with my cousin, he'd take one look at me in the nets and say, 'Give me the strike. I'll hit fours', so that was my early contribution with the bat. Trying to get to the non-striker's end at any given opportunity. Not much has changed there, really. I bowled a little bit. I just tried to bowl straight. I wasn't quick and I definitely didn't swing it.

But I watched shedloads of cricket. I was mad on it. There was cricket on the BBC at the time, England games and county. I sat in front of the television and absorbed it. I'd go to Lancashire, too, and when I got home or to the nets again, try to copy people that I liked.

Shaun Pollock. Copy his action. Peter Martin. Copy his action. It was like memorizing the essence of it, then trying to recreate it in your own way.

You'll find that pretty much all of the batsmen at the highest level have been taught closely from a young age. Technique is so key with batsmen. The schools that have facilities often develop them. It's no coincidence, for example, that, as well as being extraordinarily gifted cricketers, Alastair Cook and Joe Root went to good schools. You need it drilled into you if you are going to have any chance of weathering the rigours of how you're examined at international level: your courage, your patience, your decision making. You really need technique as a foundation at the least. By contrast, with most of the best bowlers in the world, they're not always technically that 'good', they just…bowl. The inspiring thing is, the really good ones can spring up out of anywhere, not necessarily by design or from the inner workings of academies or systems. The challenge, once a bowler has found that natural ability, is whether their body can physically endure the demands in the long term or whether they have the discipline to do it regularly enough.

In the off season at school, between the ages of 15 and 16, I grew 30cm (1ft) taller. I could bowl a bit quicker. It was as much a surprise to me as it was to anyone else. We used a sports hall for indoor nets, where the surface was rock hard. A few of the batsmen came out a bit flustered and flushed red after the first club practice back, saying, 'You've put on a yard, you're quicker than you were last season.' I can't lie – it was a good feeling. From that day, I was encouraged by everyone to bowl quick. 'Don't worry about where it goes,' was the advice, 'just bowl as fast as you can.' I did that for about a year, with varying degrees of success. We'd have professionals come and play occasionally. Really good cricketers like Michael Clarke, Dale Benkenstein and Jacques Rudolph. I think having the exposure of bowling at these types of players at a young age really helped my development. I got two out first ball that year. Roger Harper and Martin van Jaarsveld. They were quite big scalps at the time and it was just enough of a light-bulb moment to lead me to believe that I could make it happen for myself against 'proper' cricketers. My mate's mum had the good grace to speak to the coach at Lancashire, saying, 'You should have a look at him.' That kind of thing has happened right across my career – there has always been some kind of divine intervention that just kept me going at the right time.

I spent a year playing under-17 and 2nd XI cricket for Lancashire while my school gave me time off to play games during the week. St Theodore's were brilliant to let me do it. They let me drop English to compensate and still get some A levels. Toward the end of that year I signed a Lancashire contract. I got into the Lancashire first-team squad, which was a bit of a miracle in itself. I was running in, never really sure if I was trying to knock people's heads off or get them out, just trying to get it roughly straight and thinking in the back of my head, 'I'm probably going to get found out here, but I'll keep running in until I do.' Mike Watkinson was the bowling coach at the time. He was a really resourceful cricketer in his day, a swing bowler who reinvented himself as an off-spinner later in his career and got into the England side. If you watch footage of me back then, I look like a totally different person, let alone bowler, but he had the foresight to notice something in my action. He took me to one side and showed me some really basic things about swing bowling. It was all about seam position, wrist position and, most important, feeling the fingers off the seam as the ball left your hand. It was all news to me. I'll always be grateful for that. I wouldn't say it came totally naturally to me, but something did click from that point onward. I could do it and it began to set me apart. That was a real turning point in my life.

I bowled well that first season at Lancashire and ended up going to Australia with the Academy. (At the time, The Academy was a development programme for potential England internationals before they dreamed up the lions teams.) By another slice of good fortune, everyone in the England team got injured simultaneously; I was drafted in on a typically doomed Ashes tour, 2002/3, and ended up playing in a one-day game for England that winter. I did well. I remember Gary Lineker saying that at every single level of his footballing career he thought to himself, 'I'm going to get found out here', right from school football to being World Cup Golden Boot. I can relate to that. You never know until you're there. It was getting that first international wicket that really changed something in me. Nobody could take that away. It was proof, both that I belonged there and that I could actually affect a game. It was a very addictive feeling.

Having said that, my first years in the England side weren't easy. It was at a time when everyone had become obsessed with speed, so they tried to remodel my action in order to find two or three miles an hour more pace. My run-up was longer, my load was different, it sent my rhythm off completely. It was tough because I wanted to be learning the art of bowling, I was desperate to put all my time into learning it as a forensic skill, to keep improving, but the remodelling caused injury problems, which took away the focus on learning anything at all. I began to worry about my action rather than getting in a contest with the batsman, almost as if I was self-conscious, and there haven't been many successful self-conscious fast bowlers in test cricket. At least on the field. There is so much information in cricket, so many numbers, that when it's not going well, you tend to get blinded by it all. You can't move anywhere for seeing pitch maps of your last spell that look like someone has machine-gunned paintballs on a cricket pitch with no specific direction whatsoever; or diagrams of batsmen's hitting ranges, letting you know that you have been spanked around the ground 360 degrees, as if you weren't painfully aware the first time. There's something quite scarring about holding a ball, running in with it and watching it being launched into the distance by some bloke who's just stood there, then having to do it all over again. It can definitely be humiliating at times.

I look at it as something that I needed to go through. If anything, it maybe helped me realize that what I had been doing before was right, before I had been taught properly, and that I should go back to what was instinctive. The mental side of the game has always been a big thing for me. I used to think, if I'd had one or two good games, I was due a bad game. It's taken me a while to allow myself to realize that actually you are allowed to have a good game every time you go and bowl. In turn, too, there was a time when I'd really tear myself up for bowling badly. I couldn't let it go. I've slowly learned to give myself a break. In the last five or six years everything has fallen into place. My action and skills are as good as they have ever been and I feel really confident bowling in all conditions.

People talk about the ball being on a string. Bowling in the last few years, I have absolutely loved it. Sometimes there are these amazing passages, where everything is so synchronized, all the years of practice have built up in you so that it's as if it is happening despite yourself. You hear songwriters talk about writing a song in ten minutes, but having had to carve away at the art of it for ten years in order to give themselves that moment. I think it's relatable. There have been moments when I'm in the middle of a spell where it's almost a bit blissed out, showing off a little bit, just performing the whole time.

That habit of always watching and always learning has never left me, really. I still feel like I'm learning all the time. When Vern Philander toured England with the South Africans in 2017, he was bowling at 78 miles an hour – not very fast by fast-bowling standards – but was unplayable. I learned a lot. Then I'll watch Dale Steyn and try to bowl quicker and swing it. I never stop watching. One thing in this England team we've definitely talked about is that one player in a million, a Flintoff, a Stokes, can just turn up and turn it on; most people need to put in a lot of work. Studying the game, for me, is the easiest thing to do. I'm on the ECB app every day; I watch most of the county cricket wickets on there. You've got to embrace it. To this day in the nets I'm trying to hold the ball in different ways to see what it does. You have to retain that spirit of curiosity and exploration, otherwise the game will move past you pretty quickly.

Admittedly, there are mornings when I get up and think to myself, 'I don't know if I want to do this today', but the minute I get the ball in my hand that's gone and I'm into it. Once I'm there, you'll do well to get the ball off me. I remember bowling in the Ashes at Old Trafford in 2013, the test we won that went really close, and I bowled a 13-over spell (that's more than twice what you'd usually be expected to bowl in one stint). Everything was hurting, but I just kept going. There are times when the responsibility and the battle carry you further than you imagined you could go. Similarly in 2018, in an exhausting series that had been touch-and-go throughout the summer, I was bowling in the last test at the Oval. It suddenly looked as if India might chase the runs down against all odds. I'd bowled all day and had started to just try to contain them. Joe Root tried to take me off to save me for the new ball, but I convinced him otherwise. I couldn't stop. It culminated in me taking the final wicket with the last ball of Alastair Cook's test career to become the highest wicket-taking fast bowler ever. I'm glad I kept going.

There's nothing better for me, even if I don't get wickets, than bowling 25 overs in a day and when I'm walking off, everything is killing. You know it's going to hurt like hell when you get out of bed in the morning, but you've worked for the team to help them win a game of cricket. It does feel sometimes that you're in so much control, you know exactly where you will land the ball. There's such a rhythm and certainty with every step of the process. It's quite a Zen feeling. I think I will bowl after I retire, without question, even into a baseball mitt at the other end of the wicket. Seeing the ball do what I can make it do, I love that. I'll never get tired of it.

Deliveries

OUT-SWINGER

My stock delivery is an out-swinger. I'm looking to swing the ball, as late as possible, away from the right-handed batsman. The later it moves, the better chance of the batsman misjudging the ball and playing down a slightly wrong line. I'm trying to get batsmen out caught behind in general, either by the wicketkeeper or in the slips, or from leading edges into the off side if they are playing more expansively. The out-swinger is the ball I've relied on most to take those early innings wickets, but it also becomes the foil that every other ball is a variation and deception on.

In order to get a ball to swing, a team will be at pains all day to keep one side of it shiny, making sure it's smooth and constantly polishing it. The other side will become duller and duller throughout the day, meaning there's a marked difference between the two sides as it gets older. In my grip, as is classic with out-swing bowling, the shiny side will be pointing toward the leg side (to a right-handed batsman). The seam will be tilted slightly to second or third slip: it's as if I'm angling it in the direction I want it to take. Obviously, with different balls and conditions, I will constantly be tinkering with this angle. If it's really swinging, sometimes I might want the movement to be less exaggerated, so I'll make the seam slightly straighter. When it's tougher to move the ball, while the ball is neither new nor old in the subcontinent for example, I might tilt it more to try to get anything I can out of it. Often, I'll be using slight variants to a batsman, in an effort to constantly give them something to think about in terms of the degree of movement.

OUT-SWINGER

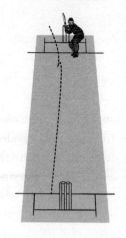

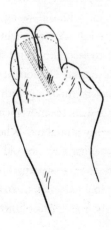

The wrist position is key. I keep it really rigid and cocked so it gives me that 'flick' at the end of the release. The flick gives you pace through the air and liveliness off the wicket while keeping the seam in an upright position. The last detail for classic swing bowling is thinking about which finger will be touching the ball last as you let go. A lot of people use their middle finger, but I think about my index finger leaving the ball last. It helps to give me the feeling of pushing the ball into the right-hand batsman, but also seems to allow the ball to swing later. Another trick to check that the ball is sitting right in your hand as you run in is that you shouldn't be able to see your third and fourth fingers in your grip. In conventional swing bowling, both with out- and in-swing, my fingers are touching the seam and are quite close together. They're not quite making contact, they're ever so slightly apart, but they are both touching the seam. The feel of both fingers touching the seam and your fingers then releasing the ball off the seam are really important for swing.

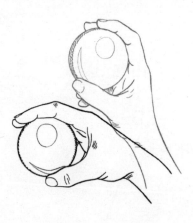

There's another common theory that the reason people swing the ball one way or the other is through the action at the crease. I'm not really a subscriber to it. My belief is, if a bowler's wrist position is really strong, they will be able to swing the ball *despite* their action rather than because of it. The old received wisdom would be that a front-on action swings it in, a classic example being New Zealand's Shane Bond. But that doesn't account for Malcolm Marshall, Andrew (commonly known as Freddie) Flintoff or Steve Harmison. They were all famously front-on in their approach but shaped the ball away.

REVERSE SWING

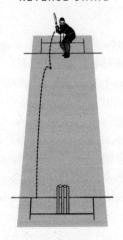

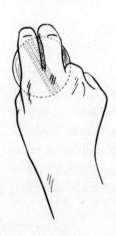

If the ball has started reversing, when it gets old (which literally means reversing, so an in-swinger will go out and vice versa), there's no real difference in the grip. The trap with it is that once bowlers see it reversing, they'll get stars in their eyes a bit and try to bowl really full. It's like an ego trip, seeing it reverse at yorker length, and has become the go-to tactic because that's how the Pakistani greats like Wasim Akram and Waqar Younis did it when it was innovated. Obviously if you can bowl it at 95mph like Shoaib Akhtar, great. But for me, I still try to reverse it at the same length.

The key thing with bowling these balls is how they feel. Bowling is so much about intuitively knowing what feels right and wrong and being able to understand it innately. I can often feel that the ball is right or wrong before it's landed. You get a sense for it. That comes with practice and constant trial and error. I'll try to bowl it consistently in a net practice, getting as close as I can to the intensity of a match situation.

IN-SWINGER

When I'm bowling an in-swinger, I'm obviously trying to do the opposite to the stock delivery, so the ball should shape back in to a right-handed batsman. Often I'll set up a batsman by bowling a number of out-swingers, letting them see the ball swing, and when they are in the mindset of pulling out of shots so that they don't edge the ball moving away from them, I'll throw in an in-swinger, which, if executed well, will jag back in late and hopefully pin them on the crease LBW or bowled.

IN-SWINGER

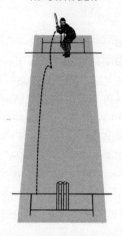

You bowl an in-swinger on the same principle as an out-swinger, but with the opposites applying. I'll tilt the seam toward an imaginary very fine, fine leg. As with the out-swinger, dependent on the movement and who I'm bowling at, I'll occasionally tilt the seam square or straighter. Instead of the index finger, with an in-swinger I think about the middle finger coming off the ball last. Again, that helps the ball feel like it's going to move later. The wrist position, again, is key. You still need that locked, cocked wrist, to keep the seam up and the ball going in the right direction. I know it's sitting right if I can see more of the back of my hand than I can with the out-swinger when I run in.

OFF-CUTTER

In overseas conditions, or usually in the second innings of a game in England, when the pitch dries out and starts to take a little bit more spin, I bring in the cutter. It's something I've evolved over the years. I became conscious of having some resources when the ball wasn't swinging. Glenn McGrath used to say, 'Imagine the ball isn't going to swing, prepare for that, then it'll be a bonus if it does.' I was mindful of that. It's become a way both of surviving and of providing the impression of variation when a batsman has begun to get set at the crease and conditions are unsuited to me, as well as becoming a legitimate wicket-taking delivery in itself.

I try to jam my index finger into the side of the seam. To the batsman, if they are watching my hand in my run-up, it looks like I'm bowling a 'normal' ball. At the last minute, on release, I'll pull my index finger off the side of the ball the way an off-spinner would. It's important still to bowl the ball fast – you need it as much as possible to give the impression of being your stock delivery. Mine will come out slightly slower, maybe 78–80mph, compared to my out-swinger, which is roughly 83 these days. I'm hoping for the ball to grip on the surface. It will rarely spin sideways, the way a spinner might turn the ball on a conducive pitch, but I'm looking for any kind of movement. It might just grip slightly and, combined with the subtle change of pace, it can be quite a creative way to take a wicket.

I got Che Pujara with an off-cutter at Trent Bridge in 2011. He played through the shot early and was caught at mid-wicket by Ian Bell. Similarly, I got Shane Watson in the Ashes, caught and bowled. It's great when a plan comes off. The off-cutter works particularly well for batsmen who are going hard at the ball, so if it stops in the pitch and comes off a little slower than they're expecting, they can either chip it back to you for a caught and bowled or knock it to one of the fielders.

If I'm throwing in cutters, I'll usually have a catcher in at mid-wicket or extra cover. Sometimes both, because it brings in that leading edge or false shot. It works really well to left-handers, too, as then it's spinning away from them. I got Chris Rogers like that in an Ashes test. I had two cover catchers in specifically for it. I've bowled it both over and round the wicket, as it's something you have to be a bit instinctive with. Sometimes I've even loaded the field 7-2 on the off side for it.

LEG-CUTTER

Like the difference between in- and out-swing, this takes on similar properties to the off-cutter but applying the opposites. You're trying to get the ball to pitch and 'spin' away from the right-handed batsman. The middle finger jams into the other side of the seam. Like the off-cutter, hiding the ball from the batsman on approach, at the last minute I pull the middle finger over the side of the ball.

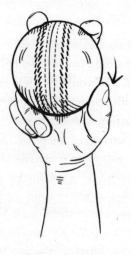

Stuart Broad is brilliant at this – it's one of his best deliveries. It's something that I've learned from him. It actually famously got me the wicket that took me past Ian Botham's record at Antigua. It was Denesh Ramdin caught at first slip by Alastair Cook. That's quite typical of a situation in which I'd use it – trying to get something different off the ball when nothing else is working. It can be quite speculative. I'll just be looking for it to do *something*. It might come off the surface slower, or it doesn't need to move as much as a leg break, but a little bit of movement, away from the right-handed bat at pace, can very often find the edge.

WOBBLE SEAM

In almost all of what I do and try to practise, I'll be searching for perfection. The perfect seam position, the ball arcing by design – I love the control of it all. The wobble seam is set up as the antithesis. You release the ball with less precision, searching for the seam to look scrambled. It's putting it in the hands of the gods a bit. The ball might land on the surface of the pitch and keep low or hit the edge of the seam and jag one way or the other. The philosophy is, 'If I don't know which way it's going to go, then the batsman definitely doesn't.'

I release my fingers slightly, so both my index and middle fingers are on the surface of the ball and not touching the seam. On release, my wrist is less rigid and cocked, too. I'm not overly fussed about the revolutions on the ball or, as I say, the seam position – it's about the imperfection and the scrambled nature. I'm literally looking for the ball to 'wobble' slightly.

The key is landing the ball in the right area, on a comparative length to what I've been bowling anyway, so that, regardless of what it does, the batsman won't be able to do too much with it.

SLOWER BALLS

I've got a few variations of slower balls. The deception is in keeping the arm speed the same. One is like the off-cutter, but maybe 15mph slower. I'll have loosened my grip slightly. There's another one with a similar grip, but at the last minute I turn my wrist so it's facing the batsman. I'll almost be flicking it with the back of my hand.

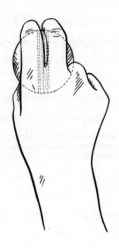

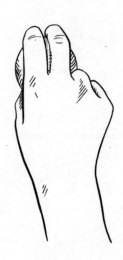

The third and final one is a knuckle ball. I'll hold the ball quite loose in my fingertips, far less rigidly than for the in- and out-swinger, and, at the last minute on release, I'll use my thumb to push the ball against the knuckles in my index and middle finger. It comes out at about 15mph slower too and will wobble in the air a bit. The trick with the slower ones is that I'll try to land them on a 'good length', a similar spot to my stock balls. That adds to the deception without allowing the batsman to pick it. It requires a *lot* of practice. I rarely bowl these any more, given that I don't play much short-form cricket, which requires a really wide breadth of variation and unpredictability to counter an attacking batsman, rather than the discipline and consistency expected at test-match level.

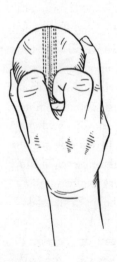

Run-up

When you're first learning to bowl fast, the classic thing to do is to run up from as long a distance as possible. I've played with people at club level who'd be running in from the sight screen and were visibly exhausted by the time they reached the crease. Cricket is a spectrum of emotions at the best of times, but the batsman would go from quaking to bored during the bowler's approach to the crease alone. It's a learning curve we all have to go through. I've actually had the same length run-up since I was 15. What a lot of younger bowlers forget is that the run-up is all about the last six steps, really. Leading up to that, it's just about finding some rhythm. You build up pace right at the end, and that's where you find your intent and direction to the batsman. If you look at some modern quick bowlers, like India's Jasprit Bumrah or our own Mark Wood, they both have very short run-ups. It's very explosive over a small distance. It's gone some way to dispelling the myth that fast bowling is dependent on really long run-ups.

Lots of people use targets on the pitch. I've always liked using a stump. You get variable lengths – the ball bounces less or more on certain wickets or pitches – so I just try to keep my focus on hitting the top of off stump. That's my aim, and the line and length tend to vary a little to accommodate it.

As a swing bowler, too, I'm using everything I can that might give that hint of difference or subtle variation that might double-bluff the batsman. One of the things I've learned to use over the years is different arrivals at the crease to help with angles. A lot of bowlers will arrive in the middle of the crease as their stock delivery, and then go slightly wider for variation. Arriving wider is especially useful if the ball is swinging a lot: it gives the ball an opportunity to hoop back more as well as swinging later. A less common trick, which I've found helpful in the last few years, is arriving really tight to the crease. Dale Steyn will do it, arrive really tight to the crease and swing it away. Again, it's about creating as many angles as you can without it being too obvious at the other end.

When I'm running in, there's a lot of pressure on my front leg when it lands, so I tend to need my front foot to get good amounts of grip. In England, the pitches are pretty accommodating. The foot holes at the crease give you enough support to land, but are soft enough to provide some give. Overseas, foot holes can get dusty and don't give you quite enough or, worse still, they can be so hard in Australia that they feel totally unforgiving. Once you notice it, it's just one of those things you have to be aware of and adapt to. When a foot hole becomes too dusty, I try to make a mental note and then have it in the back of my mind to fall just before or inside it on delivery.

In a test match, once I've bowled a ball, I'll be analysing it as I walk back to my mark. I'll be asking myself what was wrong with it, whether it was too short, full or wide, then I'll think about how it felt coming out of my hand. Once I've reached the top of my mark, I might have a look around the field, just to check all the fielders are in the right position. I'll glare around at a few and gesture if they aren't, then I'll stop and really quickly visualize to myself the series of events that are about to unfold. When I'm running in, it's as if I get immediate tunnel vision. Everything changes. I'm homed in on the pitch. My peripheral vision becomes narrower, but sharper too. I'll have a little bit of an eye on the crease line, a bit of an eye on the batsman and, really importantly, my mind will be free of any specific technical detail. It's all feel and rhythm. At the last minute, on release, my head will go down with the effort. I'll actually lose where the ball goes in a split second, then my head will come back up and I'll pick it up again.

Conditions – the Science of Swing

The received wisdom with swing bowling is that the ball is more likely to swing in overcast, cooler conditions. The theory supports why England has traditionally produced so many swing bowlers. The thing is, not to blow the whole thing open, I'm not a big believer in cloud cover, really. I've swung the ball when it's 35°C (95°F) and there's not a cloud in the sky. On the other hand, I've swung it when it's 8°C (46°F) in England. One thing I've tried to steel myself with is that, even if there *is* some truth in the theory, you can never be sure what the ball is going to do, so you never assume anything. There are a lot of opinions. Even the scientists that get involved still don't seem entirely clear on why it happens. One observation of mine, though I don't stop to discuss it with anyone, is that it will be more conducive to the art if it rains and then the sun comes out straight after. The rain will create moisture in the ground, then with the sun the moisture will obviously be in the air. It's like the pot of gold at the end of the rainbow. I feel like that's when it moves around more. My only real science, though, is on the morning of a test: I ask people who have bowled in the morning warm-ups whether it's swung or not. That will dictate how I decide to go out and bowl. I don't know for certain, though. In truth, I don't think anyone does.

The received wisdom of 'reverse swing' is a little more precise, I think: if you keep one side of the ball rough and one side smooth, it will start reversing as it gets older. There is some empirical truth in that. When one side of the ball gets really rough and abrasive, and the ball is old, it does tend to happen. It's mainly in hot countries; for the conditions to be abrasive and dry to in turn affect the ball, the climate usually needs to be abrasive and dry too. For example, often in England, where it tends to rain and the outfield can be quite lush, even damp, the ball doesn't get an opportunity to become dry enough. You need scuffs on one side that almost look like little flakes of leather coming off the ball. It's why you'll see fielding teams throwing the ball into the ground at the wicketkeeper (the ball won't tend to get dry enough in England to do that, so you will be more likely to see it in hotter countries). It's a matter of doing anything you can to exaggerate its condition.

In India, the new ball swings, then it's over to the spinners before the ball becomes old enough to reverse. That's where I tend to come back in. In 2012 I bowled Sachin Tendulkar with one that reversed back in. The ground went totally quiet. You could feel it in shock. It wasn't quiet in my head. I couldn't believe it had happened.

· · · · W

Game Preparation and Setting Up a Batsman

The day before a test match, you usually get the opposing team-sheet in. When I do, I'll visualize the scenarios I imagine will come up in the game. I'll look at the six or seven top batters in their team and bowl at them in my head. Firstly, with the new ball, I'll be pretty clear about the fields I'll set and the plan to get the top three out. Generally, there is a standard field we set and then there are certain things we look for, perhaps a certain field position for a certain batsman. Little quirks. We had one to Pujara in the summer of 2018. We noticed he hit a lot of balls specifically 10 yards short of square leg. So, we put a fielder there and must have saved 30 or 40 runs in the course of the series. It may not have taken his wicket, but all that kind of thing helps build pressure over a series.

Then I'll think about second or third spells, bowling to the middle order with a slightly older ball that might not be doing as much. It's almost like rehearsing the whole thing. I find it really important to go through most eventualities, so I'll work through being hit for boundaries and not being able to make the breakthrough early. That way, if it is tough, I won't be flustered into reacting uncharacteristically, because I'll already have catered for it in my head. It doesn't stop you getting a bit grumpy, though, when it does go slightly off piste, I'll admit that. That part isn't foolproof.

Quite often, when the game's happening and once I've planned, I'll feel prepared enough to go on feel and instinct. I'll have an idea of how I'm going to get someone out. Certainly, in the first 20 balls of their innings, I tend to target that. I'll have a plan in my head, but you can't be too rigid with it. If the pitch is too flat, you can't have five slips just because someone edges the ball a lot, for example. Quite often, for me, if the ball swings a lot, it's easy to get giddy and think I'm going to bowl 'out-swing, in-swing, out-swing, in-swing'. But if you stick to something like that you can mess your lengths up a bit without getting into a rhythm. It's about patience and set-up. I might bowl an in-swinger early to a right-hander, beat him and then not bowl it for a few overs, so you feel him fearing it but not knowing when it's going to come.

With the really great players, the challenge is that you have to focus so hard on bowling the perfect ball every ball. Whatever you are trying to bowl, it has to be the perfect version of it every time. With other players, you might be able to bowl an imperfect one and they don't quite latch onto it. With batsmen of the calibre of Virat Kohli, Sachin Tendulkar and Steve Smith, really special talents, you know they can hit a good ball for four as well, so you've got to make sure you're on the money every single ball. For me, with them, it's a concentration thing rather than a specific plan. You need to have the capacity to not get bored with your plan, bowling the same ball again and again.

I talk with Stuart Broad a lot about this. We've developed a really strong understanding since we were thrown into the New Zealand side as a new-ball partnership in 2008. We both responded well to being given that responsibility and we've tried never to lose sight of it since. There's a dependence on us to keep sides under pressure. We try to avoid the temptation, for example, when it's our last over, to attempt to bowl a couple of miracle balls that take a wicket. You might get clipped for boundaries and then suddenly all that pressure you've worked so hard to build is released. Whoever comes on next has to recreate it from scratch. It's called 'getting out of your spell.' That's something that's really important to us. There's lots of conversations between us and not just the senior members, but the entire team. We talk pretty much every over. Even if it's to give you the confidence that you're doing the right things. Sometimes you're just running over the plan, looking for reassurance that it's right. Anyone can get involved. They can say, 'I don't think this is working, try bowling round the wicket.' That kind of thing.

As a young bowler, I hadn't bowled much even in county cricket when I started playing for England, so I was looking for all the help I could get. To be fair to myself, there aren't many 20-year-olds who come in and say straight away, 'Right, this is what I want'. Sam Curran is a bit of an exception to that. It's telling that he had played county cricket for a few years by the time he arrived on the international scene and he was pretty clear about what he wanted with his field settings. It was impressive. When I was his age I was looking for as much guidance as I could get. My first over in test cricket went for 17 runs because I didn't really know what field to set (*see* First Wicket in Test Cricket on page 52).

Aches and Pains

Running in and bowling fast for a living takes a huge impact on your body. I know I've already moaned about it once, but at the point of delivery, a bowler has around seven times their body weight going through their front leg. A small grace for me has been that I am relatively light at around 80–85kg (175–185lb). It can prove harder for the heavier guys. I don't think it was a massive coincidence that Freddie Flintoff, who's both taller and broader than me, had to retire really young, at 31, with ankle and knee problems. It happens to so many.

I've rarely ever bowled pain free and, to state the obvious, it doesn't get any easier the older you get. Fortunately, I have quite a high pain threshold, so I've always just found a way to get through it. There's a skill in knowing how your body works. I've very rarely, if ever, bowled at 100 per cent fitness either, but you begin to pick up on what general bowling pain feels like and what is the beginning of a tear or a serious injury. I used to notice something that didn't feel right but bowl on because I was so desperate to keep playing. I've had to be a bit more mature about it in recent years. Sometimes, as much as you want to bowl, you have to allow yourself to rest, and it is pretty common that I'll be bowling slightly within myself, knowing I can push myself harder if required. On bowling days I'll take Ibuprofen to get through the workload, but in general that's something I try to avoid.

I had back pain throughout six one-day games we played against India in 2006. The medical team thought it was just a bit of a stiff back. I carried on playing for the entire series. When I got home, I had a scan that showed I had a stress fracture. One of my vertebrae had cracked. I had to wear a corset thing for six weeks. I couldn't do anything. No gym, no cricket, no running. I was out for nine months. That was a bit of a pain in the a**e. It was ironically caused while I was trying to change my action to something that would supposedly be safer. As soon as I got fit, I just went back to what I knew, and it's served me pretty well since, bar a shoulder injury a couple of years ago that prevented me from doing simple things like brushing my teeth or putting a shirt on for a while.

I've been really lucky in general that I've had structured strength and conditioning programmes my whole career. It's crucial for me to have a strong core, as there's so much emphasis put on looking after both my legs and my back, the areas I know will be under the most stress. I'm always running, and I find doing interval sprints really useful. It gets you into the habit of recovering quickly when there are brief moments of rest during a spell, in between balls or overs. It's pretty brutal then.

The time it can really strike home how much physical exertion you are putting into your bowling is when you're not playing. I don't bowl that much in the nets any more. I used to be pretty obsessive about it, but it began to put too much workload on me. In practice these days I bowl for five or six overs flat out and then I'll do interval sprints followed by some drills. The drills are to help with the important parts of my action. I'll run up from a few paces and concentrate on small things, like my wrist position and my front arm going at the target. It helps that I've got that locked in, so it's one less thing to worry about in a game situation. Then the rest of the preparation is in the head.

CHAPTER 4

In the Dressing Room

You're always walking that tightrope

between really serious intensity and

total silliness.

Changing Rooms

It took me a while to find my place in it, but I now consider the dressing room my natural environment. Apart from home, it's the place in the world I'm most comfortable. The first rule is you need to hand your phone in. Our security guy, Reg Dickason, collects them all in the morning and you don't see them again until the last ball of the day is bowled. It does tend to give test matches a slightly timeless quality. It's an understandable measure to ensure that there's no in-game betting on cricket any more, but as you can imagine, 25 men being separated from their phones for seven hours a day in modern times can be quite a challenge in itself. It's as if suddenly the test match is the only thing that's going on in the world. Certainly in your world. The only outside communication is the delivery of newspapers in the morning (so we can do the crossword – I'm keen on that) and the possibility of changing the channel on the television, which is set to the coverage so everyone can see replays, but switches to *Countdown* when it comes on at teatime.

The squad will usually have practised in the ground two days before, so everyone will have found their spot and their kit will be laid out exactly how they've left it. There are some who will have everything folded, bats lined up, everything compartmentalized, and others who will have kit everywhere, manically rustling around for their shirts when the bell goes for play. I'm somewhere in the middle. I'll make sure there is a pair of boots in reaching distance that I can throw on quickly if I need to. Over the course of five days everything does tend to unravel and encroach into other people's space. It's as if, as the game takes shape, everything starts to melt into one. You can imagine the stench in there toward the end of a test match, with old kit flung about everywhere.

For the senior members, there's generally a spot that you've unwittingly made your own. I know where I sit at Lord's, Old Trafford, the Oval and so on. The new players will have to work around the seniors to find somewhere. There's no real tension over it, but sometimes you do need to give a new player the odd heads-up – don't sit next to Mo (Moeen Ali), for example, because that's where Rash (Adil Rashid) sits, and they're inseparable.

The only rule for home tests is that you need to be there for the group warm-up at 10.15. As long as you're on the field by then, anything goes, really. The batsmen can go and have a hit in the nets, wicketkeepers do their drills, spinners will more often than not have a bowl, fast bowlers will have a massage. Everyone's bombing around the place doing what they need to do.

One rule that absolutely needs to be observed by all is the drug testing. If you are centrally contracted, which the large majority of the England test squad is these days, you are required to fill in a form that tells the panel where you will be in an hourly slot on *every* day of the year. They could turn up unannounced at your house 6am for all you know. Most of the time, it's three or four of you picked out at random, in the dressing room after play or the team hotel. Because I'm inside the top ten of the world rankings and have been for a while, I tend to get picked out a lot. The 'testers' will turn up in an array of brown and beige clothing, ties tucked into their shirts. Imagine a cross between a lab assistant and a geography teacher. In the highly likely scenario you don't need the toilet on the spot, they'll follow you around like Tony Adams, man-marking you everywhere until you do. When the time comes, they'll pass you a plastic beaker, ask you to pull your pants down to your knees, like you're a six-year-old kid, and watch you wee into the beaker. That little ceremony has taken a bit of adjusting to.

With the obvious exception of the above, I don't know if it'll be reassuring or not to hear, but it isn't that dissimilar to club cricket. There's a rhythm and routine to the day. The lunch and tea rooms are often communal so, like at your local club, you can be bowling at someone and half an hour later you're queuing up for tea with them. It's just that it's not fat Gaz or whoever, it's Virat Kohli or AB de Villiers. If we're batting at lunch and not many down, I'm cashing in. It's lamb chops, double portions of sticky toffee pudding, back to the dressing room to sleep. Although Edgbaston runs a close second, Lord's is the holy grail for lunches. Prawns to start. Rack of lamb for mains. Louisiana love bite to finish. Thank you very much.

I'd say the changing room was quite a different place now to what it was when I walked in as a 20-year-old in 2003. There were guys in that team that I absolutely idolized and had watched on TV – Darren Gough, Alec Stewart, Nasser Hussain, Craig White, Mark Butcher, Andrew Caddick. The list goes on. They were all a big deal to me. I hadn't even played much county cricket by that point, so not many of them even knew *of* me, let alone anything about me. To be honest, I felt I was being looked at as a threat, and there was definitely an unspoken hostility from some. You could *feel* one or two of them thinking, 'This kid's not as good as me, I've been around for years.' I felt awkward for a year, but like a new kid at school, I just kept my head down and tried to get on with it. In hindsight, it didn't breed a particularly positive environment. When Alastair Cook became captain and our generation of cricketers that had hung in there started to become senior, we were conscious of attempting to change that. It's quite a high-pressure environment; even in a new player's first net, there are cameras everywhere, loads of coaches, everyone is watching. At county level, no one watches the nets, not even the players. The last thing you need is your team-mates freezing you out alongside it.

An example of this kind of thing came from Cooky himself in the summer of 2016. Toby Roland-Jones had just been bowling in the nets before his debut and he was obviously trying to impress. In an effort to be quicker than maybe he was, he was spraying it around a bit. Cooky came to speak to me in the dressing room and said that he had played against Toby in the county championship and that he'd bowled really nicely – ran in smoothly, mid eighties, nibbled it, swung it a bit and was a real handful. Cooky said, 'Shall I go and tell him the comparison between the two?' I replied, 'Absolutely.' As a bowler you are desperate for that kind of advice – it's not criticism, it's being kind enough to say, 'You are trying too hard. Just relax.' To hear that from Alastair Cook must have been a relief to Toby. He bowled South Africa out at the Oval that summer. That's the kind of group we are always trying to build, a communicative one where everyone is conscious of others around them. It's something that's continued through with Joe Root's captaincy.

Likewise, I think we're as close as we've ever been with the media. With Nasser as captain, it was very much us against them. That kind of siege mentality was probably a survival instinct and beneficial at the time. Certainly the senior guys around would get quite angry about what was written about them. When Andy Flower was coach, too, he made a big thing about not giving anyone any insight into our dressing room. It was referred to as the inner sanctum. He didn't want to let anyone in. Since then, though, I've enjoyed the freedom of allowing ourselves to be a bit more honest. In the dressing room these days, it is hard if someone dismisses your day when you've been running in for seven hours, but you try and arm yourself with the perspective that sport and media are like that: if you have a good day, they're going to write nice things and if you don't, they're going to tell people. That's just the way it is. Cooky did a great job with the ex-England players in the media, extending an open invitation for them to join us after play if they ever wanted. I think that helped and it's continued from there.

I've seen a lot in the dressing room. I've been in there for 16 years now. When I started, the most common paper in there was the *Racing Post*, and now you are more likely to be kicking drones out of the way, that Sam Curran or Stuart Broad have brought in to fly in their spare time. That tells you about all you need to know of how far it's come.

Passing the Time

One of the main skills you have to adopt as a cricketer is waiting around. There's so much of it. In airports, on buses, at hotels. There isn't anywhere you need to be more able to wait and pass the time both thoughtfully and productively, though, than in the dressing room.

As a team, you spend seven hours a day together, and that's just during the game. Some of the conversations you end up involved in…they can get very far down a vortex of nonsense. When the camera cuts to the balcony and everyone's sitting there, more often than not I can guarantee that the conversation isn't about cricket. It will be about football. We have a team fantasy league at the moment, with players from the past and current. It's very competitive. As it stands, Jonathan Trott is top. Last year, Stuart Broad, in the penultimate week of the season, got the most points out of anyone in the whole world. The whole world. That gives you an idea of the amount of time we have to waste. He still brings it up now. Sometimes I wonder if that's what he's most proud of in his sporting career.

The dressing room can be a hard place to relax. There's 15 in the squad, maybe 10 or 15 management, so you're always trying to micromanage the intensity levels of what you're doing and allowing yourself to stop. As fast bowlers, it isn't uncommon for us to spend the time sleeping. I've got it down. I find a quiet spot and peel away at the most opportune moment. During Cooky's last innings at the Oval in 2018, there was a lot of high emotion about, and from the way we were talking about it, you'd have thought we were all glued to every second like everyone else. Unfortunately, there's a video of me snoring at the back that proves otherwise. Cooky knows that I'm prone to the odd nap. It wouldn't have been a send-off for him otherwise.

I've become really good at going to sleep for an hour and, when batsmen get in for tea, giving them a knowing nod and patting them on the back with a 'Well batted, mate.' Like I'd actually watched it. They don't need to know the truth. Graeme Swann was brilliant at this. If we were batting, he'd cash in and have a massive lunch. Fifteen minutes after the lads had gone out, you'd see him sneaking off to the back to sleep. Then there was that famous Cook and Trott stand at the Gabba in Brisbane in 2010/11, when Cooky made 235 not out and Trotty 135 not out to save a match we'd looked certain to lose. The dressing rooms at the Gabba are underground. It feels like you're in a dungeon. So, by the time we ended up 500-1, we were all asleep for it. The entire bowling attack.

When you're not asleep you are still trying to take your mind off the game, just to give yourself some breathing space, but it can be hard because the TV is always on, with the commentary. That can be a little bit sadistic. There have been so many moments in my career when I've been sitting with some team-mates and everyone knows, if a certain guy doesn't get a score, he's going to get dropped the next game. There's not much you can say in that situation. It's really tough when you see that emptiness on someone's face when they know that's it. It's horrible. I remember it happening with Adam Lyth. He needed a score in his last innings, and while he was getting ready, the TV was obviously doing analysis and stuff. His dismissals are coming up just as he's padding up. There couldn't be a worse thing to watch as you go out to bat for your England spot. A couple of us looked at each other and were scrambling around looking for the remote to turn it off, but no one could find it. Sadly, he was out for 10 and he hasn't played for England since.

In essence, you're always walking that tightrope between really serious intensity and total silliness. The mood is constantly flipping between one and the other. But we do like to zone out, and the earpieces they hand out where you hear the commentary can be very useful, particularly if you need a bathroom break at Lord's. The toilets are more akin to Fort Knox. The walls are solid, so you can't hear anything through them. That does have its advantages, but the only issue is if you're in there, you can't hear the crowd if a wicket falls. I've been saved from being timed out a few times by having my earpiece on, knowing, thanks to the commentary, that I need to dash out to bat.

Though pranks are slightly a thing of the past, I do still look back with fondness on the days when they were popular. That was definitely a distraction from the cricket and a tool to be on your guard all day. Our security guy Reg Dickason was, and still is, usually involved in some shape or form. Ian Bell once superglued his shoes to the floor. It must have taken him a long time to do it. That was quite an interesting battle. Mark Saxby, the physio/resident DJ, had a camper van, the old-school Volkswagen, that he used to park at the school across from the Oval. Reg once filled the entire camper van with scrunched-up newspaper. Mark couldn't get into it. That was a lot of effort.

The Yorkshire team once had a phenomenon called the 'Yorkshire Snipper'. Someone would cut the toes of your socks off or the crotch from your undies. It became an epidemic. No one ever knew who it was. They ended up having a serious team meeting about it. David Byas, the captain then, said, 'We're not leaving the dressing room till someone owns up to this,' but the Yorkshire Snipper called his bluff and never owned up. There were a lot of names floating around, Ryan Sidebottom and Anthony McGrath among them. No one ever knew. Myth has it that he took on more than one identity eventually. Particularly inspired, and at the time a bit of a cheeky upstart, Joe Root brought him into the England team. You'd come back from lunch and all your stuff had holes in it. He'd be terrible at hiding it, just go bright red and have a stupid grin on his face. Now he's become a dad and England captain, things have come to a halt a bit with that stuff. I'm not sure he thought it was the right example to continue to set.

There are players I've played with who have had that special something that would make all squad players stop what they're doing; whether it was sleeping, the pranks, the football transfers, the crosswords, all of that would usually stop when Kevin Pietersen came out to bat. It was generally an entertaining innings whenever he was there. It was certainly always a lively start. Ben Stokes and Johnny Bairstow shared a very special partnership in Cape Town in

2016. Stokes got 250-odd, and Bairstow got his first hundred. That was absolute carnage. Everyone in the team became a fan for a brief moment. We just sat there in awe of it. It was brilliant to watch. When you are all there, just watching the game in silence, that's when you know something special has happened.

Clearing the Deck
(Etiquette When a Batsman Is Out)

Batsmen can be quite sensitive characters at the best of times. Dealing with one when he has just got out, though, and is still processing it, is one of the ongoing dressing room art forms. In a game where once you are out, you are out, you'd be amazed at the continuing lack of acceptance there is among the batting breed. There are some who need to take it out on something: a person, the windows, the physio table. Others will go totally mute for the rest of the day. You have to be aware, when they've got a low score, or been out in a way they're particularly unhappy about, that they've had a very long and lonely walk back stewing on it and you will be the first human point of contact since the event. The trick is knowing how to respond on a case-by-case basis.

It's crucial you know how every individual reacts. Ben Stokes, for example, can get a little bit, erm…'frustrated'. When he gets out, the whole place will clear. We've got a routine. It's effectively abandon ship. People will be manically darting around to make sure they're not in his line of sight when he gets back in. We'll shut any windows or doors that might be ajar. His spot will be totally clear. You need to give him *at least* ten minutes.

Nasser Hussain used to go absolutely ballistic. All. The. Time. Getting out was never his fault. The umpires needed their eyes checking. The sight screen was poor. Someone from the press had looked at him funny that morning. The dressing-room attendant had put one too many sugars in his tea. You get the picture. He used to lose it on the field, too. To be clear, I loved him as a captain. He could aggrieve some, but he helped me a lot at a really formative stage. He believed in me and knew how to talk to me. Being very shy, I realize now that that could be quite tough for a captain to manage, especially a shy fast bowler, but he knew when to shout at me and when to put an arm round me (though, to be fair, it was mainly shouting). I'll never forget my second game in an England shirt. Sri Lanka in an ODI at Perth. I was at the crease when Paul Collingwood made his first hundred for England. We made 258. Then we had Sri Lanka on the ropes – early wickets led them to collapse to 130 for 8. When the eighth wicket fell, we gathered for a drink thinking we were close to seeing the game out. A comfortable win. Nasser, totally unprovoked, started fuming. He was cursing, screaming, the lot. We just stared at him blankly while he stormed off to his fielding position at mid-off. I'm still not quite sure if anyone knows why he was angry. Maybe because we thought the game was won and he wanted to be professional about the job. He was a perfectionist and I guess that's another thing I liked about him. But it was an early warning sign to be very careful around batsmen.

The most famous incident I can remember was back in 2011. In search of quick runs before a declaration at Lord's, Matt Prior was run out by Ian Bell. Though Matt is a famously stand-up team man, being needlessly run out at the expense of your average can be a sore spot for a lot of batsmen, and Matt was no exception. When he returned, the dressing-room window mysteriously smashed. Unfortunately for Matt, the dressing room at the Home of Cricket is situated literally above the members' seats. If there's anyone you don't want to shower with broken glass at a cricket match, it's the egg-and-bacon brigade. I think he woke a few of them up. To this day, he still claims that he shrugged off his dismissal with grace and innocently placed the bat by the pane, which inexplicably shattered into smithereens. To be fair to Matt, it wasn't the first time I'd seen this happen. My cousin Lee, playing in a massive cup final for Burnley under-15s away at Enfield CC in the Lancashire League, got out in a way he wasn't happy with. Similar to the Matt Prior incident, Lee detailed to me how he placed his bat on the table next to the window only for the bat to bounce up off a stray glove and make its way through the glass. Strange. Luckily nobody was hurt, and the window was paid for in full. On both counts.

Back in the England quarters, there are others you might want to evade, not because of immediate danger per se, but because they won't be able to let it go. They'll want to analyse the dismissal immediately, get a coach over and be straight on the computer. Ian Bell was one of those. He'd want to know what he'd done wrong on the spot and literally go through it technically straight away. He couldn't move on otherwise. Mike Brearley, England's most successful leader in terms of dealing with characters with bespoke dexterity, famously observed that Geoffrey Boycott would need to be assured that the ball he got would have taken the wicket of any batsman in the world anywhere and there was nothing he could have done. Sometimes you have to oblige for the sake of harmony.

The last type, and easily the most entertaining and heartbreaking to observe in equal measure, is those who take it out on themselves. As a spectator sport, I am a big fan of the batsmen who will just sit there, pads still on, staring vacantly into middle distance, contemplating life. Cooky was one of those. It's like his existence was momentarily rendered meaningless in the wake of getting out. I'd sing 'Hello, darkness, my old friend' in my head while he sat there.

Lancashire had Brad Hodge, the Australian, as an overseas player for a couple of years. He would go absolutely mental if he got out. He would scream at himself, 'What the hell are you doing there?' and call himself all sorts of names. 'Are you a complete bellend or what?!' Away at Durham, he got out and disappeared. No one saw him come back in. There was no sign of either him or his kit. Everyone, knowing how hard he could take his own dismissal, was asking around, 'What's happened here? Anyone seen Brad?' We were starting to get a bit concerned, until we heard water running. We tentatively put our heads around the corner. He'd gone into the shower fully kitted up, turned it on and just sat there, helmet on still, getting soaked, staring into space. He was so fuming that he was punishing himself by putting himself under. It was ridiculous, if strangely cinematic. As a general rule I just try to avoid people. You're better off saying nothing. You don't know how they're going to react.

As anyone who plays cricket at any level will know, this kind of reaction isn't necessarily reserved to the professionals. Back in my club cricket days, if anything, it was worse. People put holes in walls, smashed up their bats or helmets in frustration. That one stupid shot too many can cause an existential crisis like nothing else in life. When I was playing for the under-17s once, a lad got out to a rank full hop; his eyes lit up and he just lobbed it down someone's throat. His dad was the umpire. When he reached the pavilion, from the pitch you heard a faint smash, then silence. He'd put the window of the door to the dressing room through with his bat. His dad made his excuses briefly and followed him. The kid appeared ten minutes later, full kit on his back, walking out of the drive into the distance. He was walking home. No lift that day. It deals out some life lessons, cricket.

I tend to be slightly less precious about the fall of my wicket, given that my job is obviously with the ball. There's not much time to contemplate because once I'm out, having batted at number 11 for the duration of a career, I'll either be getting ready to bowl immediately or I'll be the last wicket of the match. It can be quite hard, actually. In 2014 we had a tough series against Sri Lanka, culminating in Leeds. I batted for 50-odd balls, a 50-odd-ball nought, trying to save the game and, with it, the series. I got out with the penultimate ball of the match. After that I just sat there in my kit for a while. It was a small window into beginning to understand the feeling.

Having fallen in and out of love with batting so many times, I honestly thought my chance of scoring a 50 in senior cricket was long gone. My best effort was a nuggety 49* for Burnley 1st XI away at Todmorden. It was a match-winning knock. The detail I often miss out is that I opened and batted the whole 50 overs for it. It was a deeply unmodern strike rate. We made 137-6 off 50 overs and bowled the opposition out for 107! Despite my resilience at the top of the order, I only managed a few more games batting there for Burnley, so when I became a first-class cricketer I thought that elusive half-century would always be just that.

In 2014, when I came to the crease against India at Trent Bridge, we were 298-9 and 159 runs behind. Joe Root was at the other end. I don't know what was in the air that day, but we just clicked. I have to give a lot of credit to Joe, he talked me through the whole innings. He was constantly giving me advice and little targets. I didn't think about my score, all I did was exactly what Rooty told me. The next thing I know I'm in the forties. It had been years since I was in this position. My highest first-class score before this was 37. I tried to forget about it and kept listening to Joe. The shot to take me to 50 was a charge pull. I couldn't believe what had come over me. I ran down the wicket and pulled the ball in the air through mid-wicket. I tried to do a classic celebration, just as I'd imagined I would have done for Burnley that day, a lift of the bat toward the dressing room and a nonchalant look around the ground. I wanted to give off the air that 'this is what I do, please sit down and let's get on with the game'. Inside, I was absolutely buzzing. I was restraining myself from doing a lap of honour around the pitch.

We managed to keep going for a bit. I was just happy to be there. I'd done my job. We got the scores level and the team was in a good place. When the tea break came, I was 81 not out. I walked back into the dressing room proud as punch. There were cheers and pats on the back, high fives and smiling faces. I sat down for a well-earned drink, still trying to do that face that goalkeepers do when they make a world-class save but pretend they're not really pleased about it. Matt Prior walked over and said, 'Only 19 more, mate.' He was referring to the 19 runs I needed to make my test hundred, the first ton since manoeuvring my sister round the back garden on a flat deck as an eight-year-old. It became too real. I started to sweat and panic. I went back out after tea, swung hard at a half volley and nicked it to first slip. The dream was over.

That was the day I found out what kind of batsman I was. I wasn't the tantrum-throwing, locker-smashing curser. I wasn't the technically obsessed, 'let's fix it now' perfectionist. I was the guy who sits there in his full protective gear with his head in his hands, thinking about what could have been. I was moments from putting myself in for a Brad Hodge-inspired shower. Not having to dodge kit being thrown or jumping out of your skin when a guy swears at the top of his voice when standing right next to you is normally welcomed in the dressing room. But not this time. I had my head in my leather-palmed gloves for about three minutes when one of the coaching staff tapped me on the shoulder and said, 'We're out there in two minutes. Best get your bowling boots on.' These are the cruelties of batting at number 11. You're not even allowed to grieve. There are not many more soul-destroying things than having to go out and try to take wickets on a pitch you've just scored 81 on.

As much as I would love to have made a hundred, to have the record tenth-wicket partnership with a bloke who is already one of England's greatest ever batsmen is pretty special.

Speaker Politics

Music is on pretty much constantly in the dressing room during test matches. The problem is, the collective taste of England teams, past and present, has always been a bit, shall we say, eclectic. The younger lads tend to bring in chart music, new music, and there's always been the senior member like Andrew Strauss (or, these days, myself) dad-dancing to it somewhere in the background in some vague attempt at trendiness. It's quite a tricky balance. Stuart Broad, for example, is really into R'n'B, rap and grime. I've always wondered how a man like him, a gangly, geeky guy from public school, has found such an affinity with that sort of music. The fact that he wears over-ear headphones, so that everyone can hear what he's listening to, rather than in-ear headphones, suggests to me that he might just be trying to prove some kind of point.

The massage therapist, Mark Saxby, has been given the power of controlling the music in recent times. I like his taste, he loves things like Marvin Gaye and Bob Marley. He tends to try to please everyone, like a proper DJ. It's a slightly unenviable task in taking a litmus test of the atmosphere and playing the right thing. Occasionally you'll get someone yelling from the other side of the room to turn something off. The trick I've found, though, is that despite what you might think, you don't really want music that is going to work you up too much. It's not always a good thing to be getting too pumped up. If you're playing Australia at Lord's, you're already going to be in a state of pretty high intensity. It works better to have music that's going to calm people down a bit, rather than the other way around. The last thing you need is a hard-core rave. That is, unless you are Ben Stokes, who occasionally will take over and put on absolute noise. He needs fast, heavy stuff to get himself going. It stands to reason. As a general rule, the guy who's in next gets to make the call. In stark contrast, Dawid Malan, for example, didn't really like music on when preparing to bat, so we would turn it off, but there's usually a little bit of general background noise.

The Ashes-winning side of 2005, which I was involved in as a squad member, ended up anointing 'Rocket Man' by Elton John as a kind of anthem at the behest of Freddie Flintoff. He was into quite specific anthems for each series. He was captain in India when we won in Mumbai. That was a really big deal at the time. As is the norm out there, a few guys were struggling with Delhi belly, so Fred thought an apt anthem for that series would be Johnny Cash, 'Ring of Fire'. I have mixed emotions when I hear that song now. It takes me back to winning in India, one of the hardest challenges out there, but also endless nights in the toilet. 'Pompeii' by Bastille was another one that caught fire in the dressing room. I remember it being played over and over for a whole summer around its release. We did have some videos of the lads singing it in a cab home after one test win. I think they've since been deleted. It wasn't a good look. The latest album to be played constantly is the *Greatest Showman* soundtrack.

It is Ben Stokes' (thanks to his kids) favourite film and he loves to get the soundtrack on in the dressing room. As a result, this meant the Sri Lanka tour at the end of 2018 was pretty much constantly an audience with Hugh Jackman.

All these examples of songs reminding players of certain games or personal performances can go one of two ways. First, you love that song or album that takes you back to that happy place. Winning at the SCG, scoring 100 at Lord's or taking 5-for at Newlands. Or it can ruin it. Songs get overplayed or played at the wrong moment and players never want to hear them again. For example, when music came into ODI cricket, the team had to choose a song to walk out to. Our team manager at the time gave the job of choosing a song to the trendiest, coolest guy in the side – Marcus Trescothick. He decided 'Lose Yourself' by Eminem would do the trick. I've never asked him the thought process behind that one. If I hear that song on the radio in the car, I get a nervous twitch and have to change the station straight away. It's not because I dislike the song. It just makes me panic that I'm next in.

After a few years in the team, I felt comfortable enough to try to get my own music on in the dressing room. That's a real sign of you getting your feet under the carpet, when you have the nerve to choose the music. It went by without comment, which I was happy with, until one day Duncan Fletcher, our 55-year-old coach from Zimbabwe, came over to me. As a rule, he would only approach you for one of two reasons. To talk tactics or to tell you that you weren't playing. I braced myself. He took me to one side. He didn't look like he wanted to talk tactics. I was preparing myself for the worst. 'Who sings the song about the morning?' he asked. 'The Coral,' I told him. Nothing else was ever said about the matter. Five Scouse psychedelic pop cult heroes got a very unlikely new fan that day.

I had a massive thing for Kasabian. I was a huge fan of theirs in 2004. I wasn't quite comfortable enough in the squad, though. I'd just listen to it on my own all the time. My now wife, Daniella, when we started seeing each other, once said, 'Right, we're going for Sunday lunch', so I got in the car. She had 'Club Foot' on. I thought, 'That's it, I'm in love.'

Back in the dressing room, whatever I happen to have heard last will usually just be on loop in my head in the field. I was singing 'Tainted Love' by Soft Cell to myself all day against Pakistan last summer. There's always something, and all those accidental pieces of music have now become really evocative. There's a song called 'When the Beat Drops Out' by Marlon Roudette. We happened to listen to it the morning before the test against the Windies (West Indies) in Antigua. I needed one wicket to overtake Ian Botham as the leading wicket-taker for England. It wasn't something that I'd been that concerned about, but some family and friends had flown out hopefully to see it happen. So, much as I was trying to ignore it, I wanted to do it out there for all of them. I was being reminded of it constantly and I was keen to get there before it became like some kind of burden. It's quite hard when there's a huge screen at every ground counting down your wicket tally. I stood at my mark and, as I had been all day, I just sang that song in my head. I got Denesh Ramdin caught at slip (*see* Leg-cutter on page 86). It was a huge relief. Whenever I hear the song now, it takes me straight back to Antigua. It's amazing how music does that.

That's not too unusual. To be honest, there's always something bouncing around my head. If the Barmy Army are in good voice, which they usually are, you end up singing along with them. I like it. It's almost as if it's meditative. It's a method I've subconsciously developed to stay inside my own head, not worry about the crowd, the fielders, the batsmen. Just stay in control of what I'm doing. It gives a little rhythm to each day.

If we win important test matches, like we did against Pakistan at Headingley in 2018, sometimes we all stay around and play music together. We had this great night after that test, sat in the dressing room after everyone in the ground had left, passing my phone around and each person playing a song. A lot of people had stories, stopping everyone to tell them things like this was the first song they were listening to when they were going out clubbing. 'Pretty Green Eyes' for me. When I was going out, that was the song, as soon as it was being played, everyone would run to the dance floor. It was pretty much my teenage years. People would be shouting approval at each other with each tune, each reminiscing about some different moment in their life, shouting 'Get in' and so on. Until the phone reached Dom Bess. He didn't quite lock into the tone. He asked for Newton Faulkner, 'Dream Catch Me'. Twice. We couldn't be having that. We had been going out of our way to provide a welcoming dressing room to all the new players, but there are some things you just can't let fly. Luckily, the playlist is still on my phone today. If you put it on, you'll be listening to the sound of the England test team in 2018 celebrating and reminiscing with songs from their youth. Note the absence of any Newton Faulkner and spare a thought for Mark Saxby when you hear how much the tastes clash.

DRESSING ROOM PLAYLIST: 2018

Savage Garden – *I Want You*
All Saints – *Never Ever*
Natalie Imbruglia – *Torn*
Five – *Keep On Movin'*
Robbie Williams – *Angels*
Blink 182 – *All the Small Things*
The Offspring – *Pretty Fly (For a White Guy)*
Bryan Adams – *Summer of '69*
Chesney Hawkes – *The One and Only*
Keala Settle and the *Greatest Showman* Ensemble – *This Is Me*
James – *Sit Down*
Pulp – *Disco 2000*
Guns N' Roses – *Sweet Child of Mine*
The Goo Goo Dolls – *Iris*
Train – *Drops of Jupiter*
Neil Diamond – *Sweet Caroline*
Lynyrd Skynyrd – *Sweet Home Alabama*
Tinie Tempah – *Pass Out*
Oasis – *Champagne Supernova*
Oasis – *Whatever*
Baddiel, Skinner and the Lightning Seeds – *Three Lions*
Estelle featuring Kanye West – *American Boy*
Crazy Town – *Butterfly*
Pitbull – *Give Me Everything*
Johnny Cash – *Ring of Fire*
Go West – *We Close Our Eyes*

Erasure – *A Little Respect*
Bob Marley – *Could You Be Loved*
Mumford and Sons – *I Will Wait*
Matchbox Twenty – *3am*
Dolly Parton and Kenny Rogers – *Islands in the Stream*
Ed Sheeran – *Castle on the Hill*
Ian Van Dahl – *Castles in the Sky*
Kenny Rogers – *The Gambler*
Eagle-Eye Cherry – *Save Tonight*
Ultrabeat – *Pretty Green Eyes*
Don Henley – *The Boys of Summer*
Cornershop – *Brimful of Asha*
Blue – *All Rise*
Craig David – *7 Days*
Backstreet Boys – *Everybody*
Take That – *Could It Be Magic?*
TLC – *No Scrubs*

Superstitions

Cricket is riddled with superstition. It's absolutely everywhere, at every level of the game. You'll not find a dressing room without it. From playing at clubs in Burnley, to international test matches, I feel like I've spent multiple lifetimes watching batsmen put on the same clothes in the same order because they got runs that way once. I don't know where it comes from. I think an element of it is trying to retain control in a game that is so dependent on luck. Cricketers, in general, like control, which is challenging because we're playing a game that offers us so little of it in return. People will go to ridiculous lengths. They'll remember everything they were wearing, how they put it on, what they ate, how they got to the ground. It never ends.

You are exposed to it as soon as you start playing the game. When I was 11 or 12, my dad was second-team captain at Burnley. I was the scorer. I remember turning to him at lunch and asking, 'Why has that guy not washed that jock strap for 15 years?' I'd genuinely be confused as to why these grown men were behaving so strangely. The problem was, I'd think, well, if everyone else is doing that, even the adults, there's got to be something in it. I started to believe that as soon as I did well in a game, I should go through exactly the same routine and wear exactly the same stuff too. I guess it becomes part of your life as a cricketer.

While I've spent my entire career bemusedly observing people going through ever-increasingly pointless rituals and can be 99 per cent certain now that what you wear doesn't affect your performance, I can't claim to have come out totally unscathed. I don't walk under ladders, I don't walk over manhole covers and I won't leave the volume on 13 on the car radio (or six for that matter. I don't like the number six, I've never thought it looks nice). I was covering *Test Match Special* last year for the one-day games, driving to the ground with Michael Vaughan. We went past a magpie and both saluted it at the same time. Our arms went up and back down synchronized. It was quite scary.

Jonathan Trott was probably my favourite of them all. When he got his pads on, he'd do up the Velcro and undo it 15 times for each strap. It became a spectator sport for the whole team. There'd be a test match going on, but we'd be gathered round the dressing room watching Trotty put his pads on. We knew the whole process by heart. He'd have his playing shirt on, untucked, and his box would be the last thing to go on. He would rub it first for a while. I was never sure if he was cleaning it or not. Then, before putting the last, most vital piece of protection in, he'd stand there, staring into it as if he were a fortune teller looking into some tea leaves. In channelling this momentary mysticism, he'd genuinely be eyeballing the box as if he could see his entire innings in there. It was quite special. Whether it was superstition or an elaborate ritual to focus the mind, he would be really anal about his preparation before he went out to bat.

This was far from the end of this deep obsession with repetition in order not to tempt fate. On arrival at the wicket, crystal ball protective box clean and intact, Trotty would ask for a leg-stump guard, as a lot of players do. Once he'd been given this by the umpire, he would scratch a mark with his spikes that would be about 60cm (2ft) long (the norm is a few inches – perhaps 15–20cm). Following that, he very methodically and very precisely would scratch three times, then run his bat down the length of the mark, also three times. Once he was happy he'd made the necessary preparations, he would make sure the straps on his pads were fastened properly a few times each and that his thigh and inner thigh pads were correctly positioned. Then and only then would he be ready to face the ball. By this point the bowler and the majority of the fielding team had steam coming out of their ears. He repeatedly and religiously marked his guard after most deliveries, but more curiously at the end of each over, which often left the other batsman waiting in the middle of the pitch, watching him in half frustration, half fascination, for their 'in between overs chat'. He loved marking his guard so much that I've seen him get clean bowled and still scratch the mark three times before walking off the pitch. I'm not sure what the superstition was there. I mean, you've been bowled, mate. If he had been in bat for any length of time, which he often was, of course, I'd know that, by the time I got there, the crease would look like a trench. It was like carving 'Trotty was here' into every cricket pitch over the world.

Swanny was really superstitious, too. He had these socks and cycling shorts that he 'bowled well in'. He was convinced they provided some kind of divine intervention in helping him take wickets. I shared a room with him and Tim Bresnan on a tour of St Lucia. There was a washing machine in the apartment, so we did our own washing. He put all his stuff in with the one-day kit, which was red at the time. All his stuff went pink, including the lucky cycling shorts and socks. He finished the last years of his career in these pink cycling shorts and socks, just because they were 'lucky'. There were holes in the cycling shorts by the end, too. It wasn't pretty. But it didn't end there. Throughout his career, if we'd had a good day and he'd taken wickets, he'd use the same route to the ground. If he hadn't, the following day we'd take a different route to the ground. I used to be sat on some maddening detours with him just because he hadn't bowled well. He forgot his guitar on tour with him once, bowled well and never took it with him again. Like that actually made a difference.

My parents themselves aren't immune. They travel to watch me play quite often and occasionally the cameras, despite of course how exhilarating the cricket always is, will drift off and find them in the crowd. Normally the cameraman will ask them if it's OK to do so. Last year they filmed them for a while, sitting apart, a seat between them. Maybe they'd had a falling out? It happens, after all, to the best of us. The cameraman gathered the nerve to pry, 'Excuse me, Mr Anderson, do you mind if I ask why you're not sitting next to your wife?'

'I'm not sitting there. It's number 13.'

He likes to think he was to credit for my wickets that day.

Swanny had spent a lot of time in the county system, so I think that's where he got all that from. There are so many strange rituals that permeate there and, with the batsmen, they're often practice related. 'I didn't have a net before that game and I got a hundred, so I'll never have a net again.' That sort of thing. Another popular one was having ten pints of Guinness the night before a successful performance with the bat and concluding that therefore the only way to prepare was ten pints before each game for the rest of the season! In most cases only their weight would go up, not their batting average.

Batsmen are more superstitious than bowlers, definitely. There are loads of stories with batsmen. There's a famous one about the South African Neil McKenzie. While he was at Hampshire, the lads taped his bat to the roof of the dressing room as a joke when he was next in. He came out of the toilet as a wicket had gone down and began to panic, looking for his bat. Finding it eventually, he made the middle only just before he was timed out. He got a hundred. He made everyone tape his bat to the ceiling ever afterward. Apparently, the toilet seats all needed to be down, too, and they needed to be checked eight times. The Lancashire captain, Dane Vilas, has a strange thing with his bag even if he's not there. If he asks for a new pair of gloves, he'll make sure the twelfth man who brings them out zips it up leaving the zips pointing the same way. Jack Russell wore the same hat for his entire career. That's 20 years. Like Trigger's broom in *Only Fools and Horses* ('I've always had the same broom. It's had 17 new heads and 14 new handles'), the hat would have to have constant maintenance work, a job reserved for his wife, with a very specific routine including leaving it drying on a tea cosy sat on a biscuit tin. He claimed it kept the shape best that way because it was 'exactly the same size as my head'. Even after the hat caught fire in the West Indies, when Jack tried to dry it off in the oven, he continued to wear it until the day he retired.

One that has been slightly left behind by the young generation, probably quite rightly, is the Nelson. With the score on 111-1 or multiples of it such as 222-2, 333-3 and so on, the English umpire David Shepherd used to stand on one leg. I'm not sure where that came from, but I do remember Curtly Ambrose walking alongside him trying to get his cap back while Shepherd hopped back to his spot at square leg. I'm not sure what kind of voodoo he was avoiding or whether that was some kind of paying his dues to the cricketing gods.

Alongside the personally motivated ones, there are lots of habits that people develop to try to ensure the team wins. For example, if there's not been a wicket for a long time, someone will usually change the bails over, just swap them around. Obviously because that's going to change everything. We had it in Sri Lanka in 2018 – we were trying to take the last wicket to win the test match. Suddenly all the coaching staff have to change seats or go for a lap of the ground. They'll make a coffee, because the last time they did, a wicket went down. It honestly never stops. Players will go, 'Oh, I'll come off the field for three overs, that usually gets us a wicket.' If we're batting and we don't lose a wicket for a session, for example, after lunch people will say, 'Right, lads, back to your spots.' I despair at it sometimes.

Alastair Cook was quite big on that kind of thing. In Cardiff in 2009, I was in the middle for the last 45 minutes. Monty Panesar and I saved the first test , batting out for a draw. It feels a little easier than watching, actually, out in the middle, because at least you can do something about it, and your actions count. I came back and heard that Cooky had been so nervous he had been in the showers, out of view of the game, for the last 45 minutes, passing a rugby ball back and forth. Because we weren't losing a wicket, he just kept doing it. It became a thing. There were a couple of moments in South Africa a year later when we had to hang on for draws again. In one of them, Graham Onions and Paul Collingwood were left with the task. Cooky thought, 'Well, the last time we got out of a situation like this, I was tossing a rugby ball around', so we got a rugby ball, found a quiet corner where we couldn't hear the crowd noise or the television and just kept tossing it back and forth. We didn't even watch the match. We waited until six o'clock and went back up. Everyone was celebrating. We'd held on for a draw. We believed that we were due a lot of credit for that. It was a very selfless act.

Team Building

In the 1990s, all that was required of England teams was to turn up for a tour with their bag and their passport. It was, 'You're in the squad, see you on Wednesday at Heathrow.' That was the preparation. In the '80s, Beefy Botham would invite everyone round to his house, both teams, and they'd just get lashed. He had the Australians round for a barbecue and beers. The game, for better or worse depending on your viewpoint, has become more professional since. During the 15 years I've been playing, the never-ending quest for the competitive edge has meant that, as well as the constant practice, there's always been some kind of extra-curricular team-building exercise before big series. Never mind the actual cricket, I've been in a forest pushing cars up hills, eaten dry rice from cans at army bases, planted devices on cars in Stoke, sat in front of never-ending slide projections on leadership and trained with football teams, all in the name of team building. There really is nothing that people won't try in order to win a game of cricket.

Some have been far, far more successful than others.

The most intense by some distance was the preparation for

the famous 2010/11 tour of Australia. The idea for it came from the captain and the coach at the time, Andrew Strauss and Andy Flower. They had been building toward the Ashes for some years and, anticipating an Australian side we might have a once-in-a-generation opportunity to beat down under, had resolved to leave no stone unturned, literally, in the lead-up. It was kept totally secret until it happened. The day after the PCA (Professional Cricketer's Association) dinner (in which teams are wished luck before symbolically leaving for the plane), we were told, like the teams before us, just to turn up at the airport. The only difference was, we weren't told anything else. Least of all where we were going. We flew to Germany – Munich – at 4am. This was to be no cricket trip.

On arrival, we were driven deep into a forest and met by four, shall we say, incredibly inhospitable SAS guys. They took everything off us: our phones (it becomes routine as a cricketer to have your phone constantly taken off you), watches, food. It became apparent very quickly, in part because they made it clear in no uncertain terms, that they were there to 'break us down', collectively and individually, on an extreme wilderness-survival weekend that no one had prepared, let alone asked, for.

Once we were stripped of everything, we were forced to start trekking into the woods. It was as close to the middle of nowhere as I've ever been. There was nothing, no one, for miles in every direction. Split into four teams, the coaching staff included, we had to build and pitch eight-man tents that we slept in for three nights. We'd be woken up at 2am with it pissing down with rain and be made to run through the forest. It was brutal. You had to call everyone by their surname – Mr Anderson, Mr Collingwood. That suited Mr Flower – he'd call everyone by their surnames anyway. A disciplinarian in his own way, it was his supposed paradise. If you messed up ever it was, 'Drop and give me 50.' Even if you didn't, it was 50 press-ups every half a mile. Poor Steve Finn, in particular, really struggled with the whole thing. He'd already had his Haribo taken off him at the airport, which I think he was stewing about for the entirety of the weekend – he'd envisaged sitting at the back of a meeting hall eating sweets for a day. He will still willingly tell you that he has nightmares about doing the press-ups while holding bricks and with a tent worth of gear strapped to his back. If you consider that the average cricketer these days likes to dedicate any non-game time to the Xbox and room service, you can imagine what a shock to the system it was. The food was army rations. Dry packets of beef stroganoff and muesli that you'd add water to.

Stripped of any kind of comfort, there wasn't a second's rest. There were all kinds of challenges, orienteering, pushing cars up hills, a lot of physical stuff and group-orientated competitions. One day culminated in a kind of emergency army drill, building a stretcher on which one person had to be carried around while the group raced them over an obstacle course, through the mud. Being on the stretcher was unquestionably easy street on this one. KP took one look at it and said, 'I've got a bad Achilles.' We ended up carrying him around this obstacle course while he feigned a twinge. It was a very revealing trip.

Everything was somehow brick related. We'd be forced to hold these bricks out in crucifix position. Our arms would be out, wobbling, shaking, desperate to drop them and the men would be shouting, 'Keep going. Don't you dare drop the bricks. It's 12 o'clock in Melbourne, you'll be bowling, you want to give up then, too, do you?!' Monty was there, probably thinking, 'How is holding these out helping me field at fine leg on day one of a test match on a flat deck?' To be fair, though, they became very symbolic that winter. After spending two days in the field you did tend to think to yourself, 'It could be worse, we could be carrying bricks through a forest.' A lot of people at the time were like 'This is s**t' and at times it did feel kind of tedious, we'd be muttering things like 'What is this doing for me? We're playing cricket not going to war' under our breath while doing squat thrusts in the German nothingness, but it did bring everyone together. Each night we'd sit around the campfire and chat about stuff, which was actually pretty cool. I enjoyed spending time with people like Monty, who I might not see much of outside cricket, but you get to know people a lot better in those situations. We took one of the bricks and it made its way around Australia with us on tour. It was a symbolic brick. It really did work. To be honest, I loved it.

We had a lot of leaders in that team, a lot of big strong characters, and when you do something like that the leaders show themselves really quickly. It's quite obvious who they are. It's not necessarily getting on well, it's understanding each other and what makes everyone tick. That team was defined by us not necessarily being the best of friends off the pitch and being able to have a beer together, but having absolute trust in one another on it. I think it really helped consolidate that trust. I hadn't experienced that in an England team before.

Despite all that, it did end up pretty disastrously for me. There was a boxing challenge. We were gloved up and told to form a human ring. All the lads were getting picked out, two by two, matched up with someone of a similar size, similar height and everything. For 30 seconds, they'd call out two players. You'd get into the ring and basically just twat each other. Some took to it a little more willingly than others. It became clear they were at least picking out people of similar builds: Bresnan and Strauss, Swanny and Cooky, you know, fair fights. I'm looking around thinking, who am I going to get here? Steve Finn? Rate my chances. Jonathan Trott? Yes, please. I get picked out with Chris Tremlett. If you haven't seen Chris Tremlett in real life, he's even bigger than you imagine. He's 2.1m (7ft), built like an ox. I put my head down and hoped for the best. I don't know if this is how it works for boxers, because my defence that day was far from full-proof, but he hit me really hard in the ribs. It hurt a lot immediately. It was the kind of punch that had everyone forming the ring immediately going 'oooohhh' in unison. I could hear it while I continued to flay away. I saw one of the team doctors after, who was on the trip, and he said 'Yep, I think you've broken your rib'. I don't think he needed to look at it. He'd seen the fight. That was the kind of team-building exercise it was, the bowling unit left tearing each other in half.

The last night we were there, sitting around the campfire, all telling stories and congratulating each other for surviving, Andy Flower was the most broken man in the group. His face was just drained of anything whatsoever, he was a beaten man. It had all been his idea in the first place. Still, he must have been onto something, as we won an overseas Ashes series in some style for the first time in 24 years. My rib had even healed by then.

The next time an Ashes tour came around, the model had proved so successful that Andy put another one together. Supposedly for time-restraints reasons, we didn't go into the jungle this time. Still, there was no mention of what we were doing, it was just 'meet here'. I was sure it was a joke until I got there, a decoy for the actual trip, but we were told to meet at the Holiday Inn in Stoke. We turned up in our England tracksuits. The hotel was full of stag and hen dos. We were like sitting ducks. Everyone was already muttering and cursing because they were about to spend five weeks away in Australia and they'd been dragged to Stoke-on-Trent. It was a nightmare.

Again, we were met by three SAS blokes, or blokes who claimed to have been SAS, but most certainly were in the security industry now. They were probably bigger hitters than I give them credit for, but when I close my eyes to remember them, I just see *Phoenix Nights'* comedy duo Max and Paddy. Let's say these guys had a more shambolic, less drill-intense approach than the ones we'd met in Germany. The trip began in the Holiday Inn conference room with a three-hour lecture on surveillance. When they were done they said, 'Right, who's brought their driver's licence?' I stuck my hand up. Worst mistake of my life.

I was the designated driver for the entire weekend. What followed was two days of chasing 'clues' in the Stoke and Stafford area. I'd drive four other guys in my car, they would get out and do the clues, I'd wait, they'd jump in. I was the 'getaway driver'. I'd do a junction down the M6 from Stoke to Stafford. Drop the lads off. Pick them up. Drive back to Stoke. Waiting in the car. That was my weekend.

The problem was, it's quite hard to run around the north of England on a supposed incognito surveillance mission when you are doing it as the entire England squad. It was something that they hadn't quite factored in. The tracksuits were too obvious, so they had to go, but everyone ended up dressed like undercover policemen, boot-cut jeans and peaked caps. You know the way an undercover policeman screams undercover policeman a mile off, but he's also England's leading run scorer of all time. That's how undercover we were. The clues led us to Stoke city centre. I was parked in Sainsbury's car park, waiting for two of my team members to go into a pub, collect some 'intel' and get back to the car. Cooky had walked into the pub, closely followed by Jonathan Trott, closely followed by Chris Tremlett. They got recognized, obviously. So, while they're posing for photos, the 'intel' gets away. We failed that mission.

There was apparently this grand finale, which we kept getting told about, a shoot-out with paintball guns in a field. Once we got there, the lads were like, 'It's over, it's done.' We missed the whole thing, the shoot-out, who'd won, everything like that. I was trying to find a place to park. I just ended up picking everyone up and taking them back to Stoke.

Not that being the getaway driver was necessarily such a bad lot. At 11 o'clock at night, Ashley Giles and Alastair Cook had to put this GPS thing on the underside of a car without anyone seeing. They were sat outside a house, waiting for a light to go off, which would alert them that the people were asleep, then they had to plant the GPS. The lads went proper stealth, running through back fields to try to find this guy's house or whatever their objective was. Someone lost their phone in a field. Of course, I heard all these stories second-hand. I was just waiting in a car.

David Saker, our fast-bowling coach, was trying to find the pub at this point. He got lost in Stoke. He didn't have a phone and his walkie-talkie was out of range, he was just completely lost in Stoke. A police car picked him up. They thought he looked suspicious. He explained, 'Oh sod this, can you take me to the Holiday Inn in Stoke – I'm the England bowling coach.' They did. He got in his car and went home. 'This is pathetic, I'm not doing any more.' It was a pretty pointless exercise. There was no physical benefit, there was no challenging mental stuff, no leadership stuff. It was a car crash of a team-building exercise. Fortunately, I live near Stoke, so I was home pretty quick. Some of the rest of them had three hours to travel home. They were pissed off.

We got beaten 5-0 on that trip.

i Lancashire's cricket academy *c.* 1999 (I'm bottom right in case you're struggling). David Brown (bottom row, left) was Best Man at my wedding. His brother Michael (top row, centre) is now Chairman of Burnley Cricket Club.

ii Team photo taken during my first season at Lancashire in 2001.

iii My first ever test match vs Zimbabwe at Lord's, 2003.

iv/v Doing a spot of 'modelling' in Burnley, 2003.

vi Me and the England team arriving suited at Sydney International Airport for the five-test Ashes series, 5 November 2006.

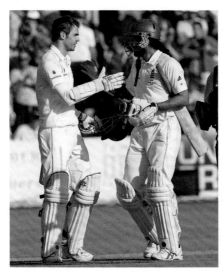

vii Monty Panesar and I shake hands after securing an improbable draw on day five of the Npower first Ashes test match against Australia at the SWALEC Stadium, Cardiff, 12 July 2009.

viii Celebrating the dismissal of Australia's captain Michael Clarke for a duck during the first test match at Trent Bridge, 10 July 2013.

ix Brad Haddin is given out caught behind on review to give us victory by just 14 runs in the first Investec Ashes test match at Trent Bridge, 14 July 2013.

x An impromptu sketch during another instalment of Swanny's 2013–2014 *Ashes Video Diary*, Episode 4.

xi Diving for my ground on 46 to avoid a run out during the fourth day of the first test between England and India at Trent Bridge, 12 July 2014. I survived and went on to make 81, my highest score on a cricket field anywhere.

xii Catching New Zealand's Trent Boult on day three of the first Investec test match at Lord's, 23 May 2015. England won the match by 124 runs.

xiii Broady covers his face in disbelief after taking 'that wicket' of Australia's Adam Voges via a great catch by Ben Stokes during the fourth Ashes test match at Trent Bridge, 6 August 2015.

xiv David Hodgkiss, Chairman of Lancashire CCC, presenting a framed photo after the naming of the James Anderson End during day one of the fourth test between England and South Africa at Old Trafford, 4 August 2017.

xv 500 down. Celebrating my 500th test match wicket (West Indies' Kraigg Brathwaite for 4), during the second day of the third international test match at Lord's, 8 September 2017.

xvi In the wickets at Lord's, 9 September 2017, this time that of Kemar Roach, in the test series vs West Indies.

xvii Cooky drops another during the NatWest test series against Pakistan at Lord's, 25 May 2018.

xviii Leaving the field with Cooky for the last time after winning the fifth Specsavers test match against India at The Kia Oval, 11 September 2018.

xix Temperature: −4°C (24.8°F). Cricket in April in England. On the balcony at Lord's for Lancashire next to bowling coach, and one of my childhood idols, Glen Chapple (note: crossword pictured).

CHAPTER 5

On Tour

Batsmen can take anything from five up to twelve bats with them. I'm not sure that's entirely necessary for me.

Packing

There are some unavoidable truths to playing overseas for England. One of those is this: if you want to go on tour, you have to pack. It's not one of my skill sets.

The first couple of tours I was picked for, I'd pack three or four days in advance. It would be a gradual process, blocking out a window of designated time dedicated to compartmentalizing everything that I needed. On day one I'd be folding all my kit up neatly, laying it out on the floor, making sure everything was pristine. On day two I'd reorganize, faff about a bit and panic slightly. Day three, start again. Day four, lay it back out on the floor, circle it for a bit, then arrange carefully in my bag. Since I've found myself as a regular on away tours, though, the precision in the process has been worn away significantly. It's got to the point that, on the 2018/19 tours of Sri Lanka and the West Indies, I just threw everything into a bag the night before. I didn't even really know what I'd brought.

It's a cyclical problem. The issue I have found is that I forget to *unpack*. I've had to get so used to living out of a suitcase that, wherever I stop, I throw my case in the corner and forget about it. If it spends most of the home tours in the back of my car, how is it going to stand a chance of being looked after properly on an overseas tour? My mindset has gradually become 'Well, I'm going to have to pack it up again next week, so what's the point of unpacking it in the first place?' When I get home, the suitcase will be in the corner of the bedroom, untouched for a good week.

It's the same with my cricket bag.

At the end of a summer, I'll throw my bag into the garage. Then, in a flash of last-minute scrambling, a couple of days before the winter tours begin, I'll go and dust it off, ready for the next outing.

ONE SET OF PADS. TICK

With pads, it's dependent on the conditions and, obviously, how successful you've been at batting as to how quickly you go through them. You can always tell you've had a horrible tour when you come back with a set of pads in the same condition they left in – i.e. they've hardly been used. In the subcontinent, you're on your knees sweeping a lot, so pads tend to wear out quicker. Even for me. But then again, I do love a reverse sweep.

TWO TO THREE PAIRS OF GLOVES. TICK

Batsmen will usually take ten. They tend to get even more sent through to them during a tour, they go through them that quickly.

THIGH PAD. BOX. HELMET. TICK. TICK. TICK

I've had the same thigh pad for 15 years. It's moulded around my leg really nicely. It feels super-comfortable. I can't imagine myself with another thigh pad, I really can't. Same goes for my box and helmet. With helmets, you're required to replace it as soon as it's been hit. So that's the only thing that ever instigates a new one. I learned my mistake after that first one-day international (look back at page 49 for a reminder of that never-to-be repeated experience). It's a proper batting one now. With your box, you only need one, don't you? What are you going to do with the other one?

EIGHT PAIRS OF BOWLING BOOTS. TICK

The general rule is one pair of bowling boots per game, including the warm-ups, plus a spare. When you go to Australia, you aren't allowed to bring any foreign soil into the country. They're very strict on it at the airport: they'll root through your bag for anything. It means that, whereas once England players would have been manically cleaning their boots before tour, these days sponsors up and down the land are getting emergency calls a week before a chartered England squad flight because we need new ones with immediate effect.

TWO BATS. TICK

Batsmen can take anything from five up to twelve bats with them. I'm not sure that's entirely necessary for me.

I don't take any balls. I know that might sound strange for a bowler. But whenever you go to play cricket, they're everywhere. During training sessions, the coach will always have loads of balls to play with. Unfortunately these days, at international level, the furniture-polished and varnished off-season ball of my youth is not really acceptable.

Some people imagine that international players have kit laid out for them wherever they go. I often wonder if they imagine us disposing of it after use as if it were unwanted litter, safe in the knowledge that the next ground will be laying out a new set in the dressing room as we speak. Sadly, for the less practically minded (which goes for many), that isn't the case.

God forbid, the responsibility actually falls on a 36-year-old man to bring his own kit.

When selected for a central contract, you're given all your kit for six months. It's up to you to look after it. It means there's a lot of emergency washing of whites pre-tour. During, it turns into every man for himself. Whereas in England you will be trying to wash your stuff at the ground, on tour it's through the hotel. Can you imagine the chaos when 15 or 16 men try to put all their white clothing through the same laundry service? It's a constant source of conversation on the WhatsApp group: 'Has anyone lost a pair of XXL underpants, Marks and Spencer?'

The white kit has become slightly less chaotic since we have all been numbered (your number of appearance for England. I'm 613).

But the training kit is no-man's land.

We're encouraged to write our names in the back of it like we're at school. Can you imagine how many professional cricketers are going to take time out of their day to label their kit with their name in marker pen so it doesn't get lost in the laundry?

Not many.

But it does mean that you'll have people like Chris Tremlett (huge) turn up with James Taylor's (tiny) trousers in his bag. Shirts will disintegrate. Whites will shrink. I've had days when I've taken them out and the three lions are pink. That's when you really know it's not your tour.

Airports

Travelling on planes is a conflicted experience for me. It's a mushed up amalgamation of my pet likes and dislikes.

I HATE AIRPORT CONTROL AS MUCH AS EVERYONE

No one likes being stuck in airports. The constant checking and rechecking. Walking around Dixons looking for adaptors for adaptors. It's something I've had to develop a kind of grating acceptance of. The actual security check, for example, I've acquired a begrudging slickness. No liquids over 100ml. Laptop out. Belt off. I know the drill by heart now. There'll be new players in the squad, though, often of an age where they've hardly travelled on their own at all, and they'll have left their electrical stuff in their bag and a deodorant in the front, setting off every alarm known to man as they go. I'll whisk past, putting my shoes back on while they're getting stationed for more checks, knowing that it'll be good for them in the long run. We've all been there. It's a kind of initiation.

It's not as full of obstacles as it once was, either. Where we once used to travel in suits, it's now tracksuits. I know that sounds like a small thing, but it does make a telling difference. You'll find that, in a tracksuit, there's less to take off in order to get through security, meaning there are fewer things that can go wrong. We're very lucky in that we get business class whenever we travel on long-haul flights, so we get fast-tracked through. I know what it's like as a father of two to go on holiday with your family, so being given this magical back route not to have to queue up for everything is something I'll always try to remain appreciative of.

I REALLY DON'T ENJOY THE PHYSICAL PROCESS OF FLYING

A lot of cricketers don't like flying. It's odd, because we do it a lot. You'd have thought that we'd have learned to get some kind of kick out of it. To this day, I just keep my head down and my fingers crossed. I know it's a subject I return to a few times, but it might be something to do with control. We like to retain an element of control in our lives, again, given that our game often offers so little of it, and flying can be a really tricky metaphorical handover of control for a group of competitive people.

The flights over with the team, though, are just the tip of the iceberg. When you are on tour there are often little trips organized on days off, where they send you off on little planes for tourist-y type things. I remember being very anxiously shuttled onto a small plane in New Zealand to be shown some vineyards. The driver was being pretty exuberant, tilting the plane when 300 feet in the air and theatrically saying, 'Loooook at these vineyards.' It was awful. I get vertigo even thinking about it again. Swanny took a photo, which he still digs out to this day, of me on the plane with my hoody pulled up over my head, drawstring pulled tight so only my nose is showing.

It's quite thematic of New Zealand. It's so beautiful you are constantly being talked into going on tiny planes to get a view. When we were in Queenstown – incidentally the loveliest place I've ever been – Andy Flower, always looking for some kind of new angle, decided we were going to do the team meetings on top of a mountain. We got helicopters up there. It was absolutely stunning. Maybe too stunning, as everyone spent the 'meeting' about our plans for the New Zealand batsmen looking around 360 degrees at everything but Flower. When the meeting was adjourned, we started to board the six helicopters to go back. Mindful of my hatred of being on those rickety things, I bided my time at the back, not particularly in a rush to get on again. The first one left and, first hovering by the side of the mountain, suddenly nose-dived down, a kind of zero-gravity 200-foot drop, before steadying its course and taking the batting unit home. It was very exhibitionist. All the rest of the team were whooping and high-fiving and talking about how they couldn't wait to be next for the adrenaline rush.

I took one look at it and told them I'd rather climb down.

There was a bit of back and forth with everyone trying to persuade me, telling me that it would be an 'incredible experience'. I said I'd be happier to be left on the top of the mountain. And I meant it. I managed to lobby enough people eventually that the last helicopter left without the totally unnecessary zero-gravity drop, and just took us home.

Slow and steady wins the race.

I really hate all of that adrenaline-kick stuff. Which does quite often leave me in compromised situations on tour, because others will regularly and actively seek them out. Once again in Queenstown, we were taken to the 'canyon swing'. Gulp. It's a 100-foot rope. You're attached to the end. It swings you out and swings you back. Everyone, again, is buzzing and rubbing their hands together, asking to go first. I can't imagine anything worse. I watched the instructors toy with the rest of the team. They were waiting and they'd count down: 'Three, two ... oh wait, no, no, no' and pretend they'd forgotten to attach them. It was funny to watch, but there is not a single bone in my body that would enjoy anything like that. Which is an issue, because there's always someone who thinks it is a good idea for 'morale' or 'character'.

I'm fine, thank you very much.

I remember being pushed off a gym box, blindfolded, with the proviso that my team-mates with locked arms would catch me. You're supposed to stay relaxed and still. My legs buckled, arms flailed and I ended up clattering into everyone. Anything like that is just awful for me. It triggers a memory of when I was 14 or 15 and ski-ing. A boy in my class got stuck halfway down. He couldn't go on. An instructor had to get him off the mountain. I thought, 'I can relate to that.'

Anyway, I digress. My point being, I don't think it's for me, really. I try not to let my head spiral into apocalyptic thoughts. We were on a long flight once with Liam Gallagher. I remember thinking, 'If this plane goes down, it'll just be in the news that it crashed with Liam Gallagher and 400 other people. The England team aren't going to get a look in.' Swanny was less concerned. He bargained to swap seats with the guy next to Liam and chewed his ear off the whole way. I don't think Liam was particularly delighted.

You do end up in some strange chance meetings with rock stars on flights. We were in the business lounge of an airport in Bangladesh once. I say 'business lounge', it was a room with seats. There was a man sitting next to us with sunglasses and a baseball cap. It was Bryan Adams. I hadn't anticipated meeting him on that tour of the subcontinent. He wasn't a big cricket fan.

POSITIVES: NO ONE CAN REACH YOU

On our long-haul flights, we're often sitting next to or opposite a team-mate. One thing I celebrate on a regular basis, with the advancement of plane hospitality, is the ability to wind a little automatic window up, so you can block them from view. You are forced to turn your phone off, too. It generally means you have an excuse not to talk to anyone for eight hours. No one can reach you. That's absolutely ideal for me.

ARRIVAL: A STRANGE MIXTURE OF OVERWHELMING RELIEF AND FEAR OF THE DOOR-STEPPING PRESS

Australia is probably the worst place for arrivals. You land in such blessed relief that you want to kiss the ground as soon as your feet touch it. The problem is, you won't be doing that in private. Down under, any sportsperson getting on a flight is an event. On a daily basis, the television is reporting some sporting personality or other being followed through an airport. There'll be a captain of a Rugby League or Aussie Rules team doing a press conference on arrival. We don't get organized conferences, we get cameras, with massive spotlights on top, following us immediately. It's such a delicate situation because you've been on a flight all day and suddenly you are balancing three bags precariously on top of each other, trying to navigate the crowd while having your every movement filmed. It's really not ideal. The main issue I'm always thinking is, 'If these bags fall now, that is going to be on 24-hour loop all over Australian TV.' You're writing your own headlines.

'Anderson drops another.'

They will be in your face with a microphone, saying, 'How does it feel to be 4-0 down, mate?' Yeah. Obviously not fantastic. It's not just the media, either: it's like a telegram has gone around the country for it to be a civilian duty to disturb you. At the end of internal flights, the pilot will suddenly say, 'Thank you for travelling with us, and oh, if you didn't know, we've got the English cricket team on board. Better luck next time.' There's always a smart comment like that. I've learned to put on my poker face as I untangle headphones and get my bag down from overhead luggage while the whole plane is laughing and pointing at us.

Welcome to Australia.

Golf

All of the England teams I've been in have been obsessed with golf. If anything, it's escalating of late. I would say 70 per cent of the current squad love playing and watching it. It's a pastime that has always been in flux as to how necessary people think it is. The early tours I went on, though full of golf fanatics, would have rules placed that you couldn't bring your clubs. It was felt that if the England team were seen boarding a flight with golf clubs, the outside world would get the impression that we were going on holiday. We used to smuggle clubs into our cricket bags.

There would be tough decisions made.

Sacrifice a bat for a putter and a wedge? I did once.

I got wise to the fact that it was what the more learned senior players did. It's about prioritizing.

In the past few years, though, the rules have been slackened. I think people have come to understand that we are away for three or four months at a time, sometimes even more, and it would be unreasonable to dictate that we couldn't have time away from cricket. It would be very counter-productive. You need to get out of the 'cricket bubble'. So these days most of us turn up for tours with one suitcase, two cricket bags and one golf bag.

On tour, without question, golf is a constant source of, if competitive-edged, relief from the pressures of international cricket. It's a bit like that time on an aeroplane that I love. Those few hours when no one can bother you. You don't need to think about anything else.

I'd say it's meditative, but I don't think, if you observed our golf days out, that the first word you'd use to describe them would be 'zen'.

There are lots of fallings out. Continual accusations of cheating. Some of them justified. You'd be amazed at the number of cricketers who have a knack of hitting their ball deep into thick forest and then miraculously finding it 30 yards away. They're very good at feigning surprise at their own fortune.

'Oh, here it is.'

You'll be scratching your chin.

'A perfect view of the green, too. How lucky am I today?' A lot of the ex-pros are also very handy with their leather wedge (shoe). You have to watch out for them kicking the ball into a more favourable spot at any given opportunity. There's also the small matter of keeping your own score. You'd have thought, cricket being such a stat-driven sport, with lots of big numbers involved, that the professionals would be able to actually count. My bugbear in golf is the nauseatingly constant response to someone being asked what their score is. They'll pause and go back with their finger, pointing at the tee. 'Erm. One …. two … three', following it on some imaginary venture to the spot they're stood in now, 'Oh yeah, into the bunker … four … back into the bunker … six.' It infuriates me. Count as you go. Others, when asked, will, suspiciously quickly, just answer,

'Four.' You have to remind them that you've just seen them take four in that bit in the forest alone. As I say, you have to keep your eyes peeled.

If it's not enough that you are forever monitoring team-mates' wanton lack of trustworthiness, it's proved quite a physically hazardous pastime, too.

I caught my calf on a cactus once.

I had to re-hit the ball off tee. Realizing I had to walk back round the steps to do it and conscious of wasting everyone else's time, I tried to hop over a cactus-heavy area to save the sighing. I landed on one. The spike pierced my calf. It literally had a hole in it. I felt as if I had it stuck in there for days, so I eventually went to the doctor, who said, 'No, you've just got a big hole in your leg.' Brilliant. Cheers.

There was a much closer call more recently when I could have done myself some significant damage. I was playing with Broady. We'd won a test the day before and I was feeling in an unstoppable vein of form all round.

I'd hit my drive into the trees.

Not to worry, I'll get out of this no problem. I had the arrogance to tell him, 'You should definitely film this, because it'll be amazing if it comes off.' I waited for him to get the camera out.

'Filming?'

Yep.

Good.

I'd planned to drive the ball very low and hard between two trees. I connected with it absolutely perfectly. I nailed it. Struck it unbelievably sweetly. What I hadn't seen was the tree trunk an inch in front of the ball. It cannoned off it at quite a rate, and the next thing I felt was a shocking pain on my chin. The ball had clattered off the trunk and smashed me in the face. There wasn't time even to know it had happened, I'd really hit it so hard.

Broady was in a bit of shock and came running over, half expecting to see me missing a valuable part of my face. I came round slowly, checking my teeth with my tongue, unsure if there were any left. I had a tiny little cut, about an inch long, on my chin. Not even deep. I saw the doctor, who said, 'That has hit you on the hardest part of your head. If it had been anywhere else, you'd have been in a lot of trouble.' I was so lucky it wasn't my eyes, nose, teeth, anything. It would have been very serious. Not serious enough for Broady not to post the video, though.

Thanks, mate.

That's the last time I've demanded anyone film me playing.

My handicap is six. It's probably the lowest in the squad at the moment, although we are fortunate in that everyone is of pretty similar ability. People often observe that it's interesting I can play golf better than I can bat. It's pretty simple. The golf ball is stationary. It's much easier to hit than one that's going toward your head at 90 miles an hour. Unless you've smashed it directly against a tree trunk, that is.

The other anomaly is that, despite batting left-handed, I play golf right-handed. I don't really know how that came about. My dad bought me my first set of clubs when I was 14. We must have worked out I was right-handed before he did that.

Before you ask, yes, I have tried to bat right-handed.

Marcus Trescothick saw me play golf and had an epiphany that maybe I'd been batting the wrong way round all these years. He found me some right-handed batting gear and we headed to the nets full of promise. It didn't go great. We both came out of that session safe in the knowledge I wasn't a right-handed batsman. I'm barely a left-handed batsman.

FIFA and Netflix

Time-killing in hotel rooms is something you need to get down as an art. There's a lot of it. When I roomed next to Mark Butcher in 2004 in the West Indies, I'd always hear him playing guitar and singing through the walls. It was quite cathartic. That's one way of doing it. Ben Stokes cut Joe Root's hair on the last tour. He's been offering his services elsewhere since. I don't think he gets many takers. I've had enough attention focused on my hair, thank you very much, without having 'the beast' at it with the closest pair of scissors he can find. Rooty himself brings his fold-up guitar and you'll hear him learning something through the walls, too. He's good in that he'll begin to incorporate it into the group. He and Jos Buttler worked out singing 'Allez, allez, allez' like the Liverpool fans while Joe strummed along. We sang it together when we beat Sri Lanka. People really buy into it.

Steve Harmison's time-wasting method was a little less interactive. He'd bring DVDs of *Only Fools and Horses* and *The Royle Family*, essentially setting up his room as close to a re-enactment of an English pub as possible. Then there are those who will try to go out and see stuff. When we were in Galle in Sri Lanka in 2018, Broady and Sam Curran dusted off their drones from their suitcases and flew them around the beaches taking photos. There's been quite a lot of technological progress since Harmy played.

One thing that has been a really communal and effective way of eating up downtime over the last decade is computer games. I'd say it's group bonding, which on some levels it is, but there are some terrible fall-outs. I've seen fully grown men genuinely become furious with each other over FIFA or whatever it might be. I'm not immune to it. On the Australia tour of 2010/11 we got into a deep vortex of Call of Duty. Someone bought an Xbox, someone else bought a projector and we'd take it in turns to deck someone's room out in pitch black, with Call of Duty sprawled across the back wall. Four-player. It would often be me and Tim Bresnan versus Swanny and Broady. I remember in the course of one game having my character killed by Swanny's and being furious with Bres for not protecting me. Bres would complain that the screen wasn't big enough to see. It was projected in high definition across the entirety of a wall.

The current obsession is FIFA. Most of the team are into it. On the floor of the hotel where our rooms are, we deck out a team room. We effectively transform a suite into a temporary common room. There are couches brought in, a TV, a table-tennis table, but most importantly...FIFA. Once everyone's had dinner, it's a race to the team room to get on it first. Winner stays on. I am distinctly average at it, but I love playing. I've found that I like playing with Mo (Ali) or Rash (Adil Rashid). The problem is, they generally stick together, even on FIFA. They're a formidable team.

On the team bus on the way to the ground, the talk will generally be about FIFA rather than the cricket. You need to stay relaxed, so I think in a lot of ways it's a protective distraction from the pressure for everyone and we've all kind of mutually agreed on it. The telling thing is that, even in relaxation, the distraction is competitive. It's always to do with beating each other at something. I think that's the nature of being a sportsman.

You just want to win all the time at whatever it is.

That's the Real Quiz

Whereas a lot of the old nights out on tour would be based around fines and drinking, we've begun to get slightly more wholesome in our group activities of late. We were raising money for Movember in Sri Lanka in 2018 and hosted our own quiz. We invited a lot of the old England players who were there on television and media duties. It was a great night.

Having people like Mike Atherton in the room did make me feel quite pressured. Myself, Broady, Jack Leach and Mo were the hosts for the evening. Mo did a spelling round. The standard within the team was, at best, poor. The best effort was three out of eight. Mo would read out a word and then go down the line asking people how to spell it. He started with 'pharaoh'. Everyone tried to spell it with an f. They didn't even get as far as negotiating the tricky a and o at the end. Nobody in the entire England squad could spell it.

I also did a film theme-tune night. I got all the songs lined up, did a bit of compering – that was a good night, too. It's been a nice evolution for me because I've always been a fan of a quiz or a crossword on tour. It's better than sitting around doing nothing. The other players have historically shown little to no interest in being involved with me. Occasionally they'll float over when I'm doing a crossword, ask for a clue and have a look at it. Cooky once got one and celebrated like he'd won the World Cup. The only one that Broady has ever got right was piña colada. He knew what ingredients made it up. He was so excited that he was grinning from ear to ear to himself as if he'd won *Celebrity Mastermind*. I think he regretted it two minutes later when he realized he was never ever going to live down knowing the exact ingredients of a piña colada.

Hiding

Especially when we're touring the subcontinent, some of the time-wasting away from cricket involves genuinely hiding. They are so fanatical over there, especially in India, that we require security with us at all times these days. One incident that made that abundantly clear was a trip to Pizza Hut in 2006. We thought nothing of it, we just nipped over the road for a Pizza Hut. As you do. We were minding our own business, comparing stuffed-crust pizzas, cashing in on the refillable drinks, when we looked up and out the window. In the space of minutes, thousands of people had gathered outside. They were pinned against the window, desperate just to get a glimpse of Monty or Freddie. Ever since then, we've had security with us everywhere.

It's the most stressful pizza I've ever had.

There are other times where you'll be playing golf in India or Pakistan and you'll hear rustling in the woods, or wherever you might have skewed your latest tee shot into. Someone from the club will have tipped off the press and there'll be TV crews hiding in the trees, trying to get a shot of you playing golf. I know that sounds like pretty niche footage to capture, but it's an example of how fanatical it is out there. Cricketers really are centre stage. Even when we're playing golf.

The problem with being an international cricketer, on tour or otherwise, is the extremity of reaction to you. It's very hard to gauge. In some places you are chased everywhere, followed around, carted about under high security. Then you'll be in a different part of the world a week later and it'll be 'Jimmy Anderson? Never heard of you, mate.' I came back from an India tour one year acclimatized to being on full alert at all times. Me and Swanny, never wanting to spend too much time apart, had gone shopping in a department store. Suddenly, from across the floor, I heard a manic and over-excited screech. 'JIIMMMYYY!? OH MY GOD!' I rolled my eyes at Swanny as if to say, 'I can't get a minute's peace these days.' We turned around like film stars reluctantly greeting our public through gritted teeth. A man was running toward me. Jesus, I thought, this guy is really keen. He must be an absolute cricket nut. He got closer. And closer still. He reached me. He kept running. I turned round, confused. Jimmy Carr was standing about 10 yards behind me, now posing for a photo.

Annnnnd Home

Sometimes you'd like to collapse in a heap when you get back from a tour, but one of the things I'm very conscious of as a husband and a father is that cricket has taken up a great deal of my time until now. When I'm away, Daniella is doing everything. The after-school trips, looking after the house, the whole lot. So when I come home, I feel a duty to do everything to give her a break for a bit. I'll try to launch right into it. I still consider my greatest skill in this life is being able to crush down cardboard to make it fit inside the recycling bin outside my house. That doesn't come easily to some. No problem for me. The cardboard bin gets collected every four weeks. By then, as you can imagine, it's pretty full. No problem. I'll literally get into the bin and squash it down. It gives you a good 20 per cent more breathing room, I find. When I'm in it, my head is above the fence overlooking the street. Just back from tour, I have the odd awkward encounter with a neighbour. I imagine them going home and saying, 'Tour's really taken it out of Jimmy this time. He's standing in his own bin.'

As I've already made clear, I'm not sure how much I believe in cloud cover as a swing bowler, but what it has armed me with is a sixth sense of when it's going to rain. If I feel the clouds coming, I'll hold up one finger, judge that the skies are about to burst and then run outside to open the bin outside the front of the house. If the cardboard gets soggy, you see, you can fit more in. It's the little touches.

I'll be on cooking duty, too. Now the kids are growing, the only trouble is they're becoming quite fussy eaters. They exist on a staple of spaghetti bolognese, steak and chips and chicken nuggets at the moment. Generally, I'll try to sneak in a Sunday roast, too.

I'll also be doing the school run. They have to have ponytails at school, so a new learning curve has been acquiring the art of those. I've got it down roughly, though I have to admit I'm nowhere near ready for plaits.

When I retire, I can't imagine myself jumping into something like coaching because it's just as, if not more, demanding of your time than playing. The cricket bag will stay in the garage and I think, to begin with anyway, I'll really relish not having to be dusting it off in a panic before summer. I'm due a more prolonged contribution at home. That recycling is not going to pack itself.

CHAPTER 6

Knowing Me, Knowing You-y

They've never missed the opportunity
to dig me out unnecessarily, so I can't
imagine they will here.

Swanny, Broady, Cooky

Since my England test debut there have been 76 other cricketers move through our dressing room over 16 years. That's a few generations and a lot of change. I've been blessed, if that's the way you want to see it, in having a handful who have journeyed large parts of the course with me. Three in particular have informed and experienced almost all that I have: Graeme Swann, Stuart Broad and Alastair Cook. Or to me, Swanny, Broady and Cooky. I know. The Brains Trust in those England sides is never going to win any awards for imagination with nicknames. It's a wonder they didn't ever call me Anderson-y.

Though I've spent disturbingly vast chunks of the time moaning at or with them, it'd be remiss of me not to say that I was very grateful for their presence. We've been through so much together, from the euphoric to the despondent to the surreal to the inane, most of which is detailed here. In the name of transparency, my two longest-serving bowling partners in Swanny and Broady have been given the right to reply. Don't believe everything they say, though. They've never missed the opportunity to dig me out unnecessarily, so I can't imagine they will here. Then there's a little ode to Cooky.

In truth, they are three of the greatest cricketers ever to play for England and I'm not sure I'd have lasted half the distance without any one of them.

Graeme Swann

60 tests

255 wickets @ 30.00

1370 runs @ 22.1

I first met Swanny at a PCA dinner in 2002. His brother Alec opened the batting for Lancashire and we got on well. We're pretty similar characters, quite dry and not always men of many words. The opposite of Swanny. The introduction was made, but I didn't really need one. Even then, years before he'd made his name as an international cricketer, his reputation came before him far and wide. The best, most diplomatic way to describe it is that the county-cricketing community, either through personal experience or folklore, all knew Swanny was quite a lot to absorb in quite a short space of time.

In the winter of 1999/2000 he had gone on Nasser Hussain's side's tour of South Africa with a new-look England squad. They were aiming to reboot the national DNA with disciplined and dedicated cricketers. God knows what they saw in Swanny. That tour, by his own admission, was a bit of a disaster for him in terms of the cricket.

He was too young (not quite 21) and too much of an upstart. In his teens he'd made a sliding-doors decision between music and cricket and he saw this tour as a kind of vehicle to practise some of the rock 'n' roll antics he'd robbed himself of. Phil Tufnell, who won't have been the most fantastic role model in terms of taking things seriously, was his senior spinner, and Swanny's incessant piss-taking really wound the leadership up.

I think they realized their mistake pretty quickly. Duncan Fletcher, new coach and looking to really drive home this new disciplinarian ethic, had a (not particularly popular) rule that if you weren't at the bus one minute before leave time he wouldn't wait for you. That just wasn't suited to Swanny's outlook on life. On the morning of the Centurion test, having already inevitably been late once on tour, Swanny was not there at 7.59 am for bus call. The coach left without him. Suddenly aware of how much trouble he was in and in a state of blind panic, he blagged a lift to the ground with the photographers. The driver, not a hundred per cent taken with the first two requests to 'chase that bus', ended up being persuaded to drive down the hard shoulder of the motorway in a bid to do some damage limitation to Swanny's impending disciplining.

As they were racing down the slipstream of the motorway, they reached the traffic, which had come to a total standstill on the way to the ground. On the hard shoulder, meanwhile, in a lane of his own, Swanny was darting past all the static, beeping vehicles. Eventually, they passed the England coach. Most people would have kept their head down, got there and got on with it. Swanny took the opportunity to climb out and gleefully double-arm wave to the England team on board. First to Michael Vaughan at the back, who laughed, then to Nasser and Duncan Fletcher at the front, who didn't. The way he describes it, daggers don't even come close. They wanted him dead on the spot.

He was first at the ground.

When the others got there he was tapping his watch, saying, 'What took you so long, lads?'It was typical of Swanny that without playing a minute of competitive cricket on the trip, his constant pranks and jokes meaning he was condemned to twelfth-man duties for the entirety, he ended up right inside not only the biggest moment of the tour, but one of world cricket's defining moments. It was that same Centurion test. There was a lot of rain and the game seemed to be idling to a draw. At the time, when games were doing that, one captain or the other would send a message via the twelfth man, to try to set up some kind of declaration in order to force a result. It's like bargaining: one captain offers to set you a target of 280 in 60 overs and the other sends a message back saying, 'No, we'll chase 260 in 80 overs', or whatever the case may be. You go back and forth until you have a deal. In this subsequently earth-shatteringly historic test match, Nasser's twelfth man and therefore messenger happened to be the deeply-in-the-doghouse Graeme Swann.

Nasser sends him to the middle with a message for the South African captain, Hanse Cronje. Swanny runs out there.

'Hanse, Nasser says he'll chase 340 in 70 overs.'

Cronje, with a smile on his face, says, 'We'll set 260 in 65.'

Slightly confused and thinking, 'That's not how a negotiation works', Swanny runs back with the message. He delivers it. Nasser is absolutely livid. 'Swann, can't you take anything seriously?! This is a test match, for f**k's sake.' Swanny, a little in a catch-22, pleads innocence: 'No, no, that's honestly what he said.' Nasser ignores him and sends him back: 'OK, tell him it's 310 in 75.'

Swanny runs back out. '310 in 75?' Hanse, again with a slight smile, says, 'Tell him 265 in 70 overs.'

Swanny runs back in. 'Nass, you're not going to believe this! The deal is getting better and better!' Nasser goes absolutely ballistic again, screaming at him 'What the f**k's the matter with you, Swann?' It was the definition of the boy who cried wolf.

He was telling the truth. But he was out of favours. Nasser sent out Gavin Hamilton with the new message; to Nasser's genuine shock he came back with the same, even slightly improved again offer: 260 in 70 overs. It turned out that, although in the immediate aftermath Cronje received plaudits for breathing life into a dead test, he was match-fixing. His reward was a leather jacket. The rest is a different story for another time, but it's very typical of Swanny that he found himself in the middle of a storm like that. When it came out years later about the match-fixing, Swanny was still being kept at arm's length from the national side. He was thinking, 'A different vehicle to the ground. The messenger. I could be the mole! The kingpin's runner. I'm going down. I didn't even get a wallet or a nice belt, let alone a leather jacket.'

After that, it was back to county cricket and winding people up. I think Swanny would have been happy with that, too. It took the passing of the Hussain/Fletcher regime for him to get another look in. Being one of those people to whom things just happen, though, he did get his chance again, in India, and he really took it. Having waited that long for his debut, he told me that when he got the ball in his hand it felt like a ping-pong ball, like he couldn't grip it. He was hit for four immediately, laughed it off and then got Gautam Gambhir and Rahul Dravid out in the first over. His first over of test cricket. In India. It was pretty stunning. I was delighted. I knew Swanny was going to be around a while from then on and there would finally be someone I could share some music tastes with.

That immediate success instilled in him a confidence that never wavered, at least at surface level, for the rest of his career. From that moment on, he decided that his mentality was going to be, 'This is a game of club cricket and I'm better than you.' He could assert control over batsmen through sheer force of personality. Taking wickets in his first over would become a habit, and it wasn't by accident. He used to say, 'If I don't get them out immediately, they'll work out I haven't got anything else.' It was this sort of slight self-mocking, but also cockiness, that made him such a successful spinner.

Even that, to be fair, undersells his ability. It was really telling that once he retired, we all suddenly appreciated tenfold how much balance he had given the side. We became the number-one side in the world while he was playing, we won in Australia, we won the T20 World Cup – we beat everyone, and a huge element of that was the balance Swanny gave us. As a seam bowler, trust me, you very much appreciate it when there is a bowler who can tie up the other end all day. Swanny could do that. He might have dismissed himself as a glorified club spinner when he wasn't in the wickets, but it was huge for us, to be able to rotate at the other end and keep pressure on teams. He was the best spinner I ever played with, for sure. He had the all-round ability, but was a great thinker on the pitch, too. He'd bowl balls that would turn batsmen inside out, particularly left-handers.

Not that his return to and subsequent permanence in the England side indicated a particularly obvious change in attitude when it came to messing around. If Duncan Fletcher had banished him, it's fair to say that the coaches who succeeded him, though finding far more productive ways of embracing his talent, would occasionally have felt that Duncan had a point. I remember in 2009, a West Indies tour. Andy Flower had taken over as coach. We'd quite often sit around on the outfield and talk about the last game. Flower required a respectful silence when he was talking. Halfway through his thoughts on the game, Swanny farted. It was loud. To this day, the loudest fart I've ever heard. Flower looked at him, in borderline shock, then paused. Swanny apologized. Flower continued. Then reconsidered, stopped and turned back to Swanny, pointing his finger in his face: 'Actually...that is out of order, Swann...' He went very hard at him. Swanny, having already apologized, held his ground. He just said, 'I've said sorry once, I'm not doing it again.' That's how stubborn he was.

That's how it works, I guess. That stubbornness that's so lauded on the field can't be turned on and off at others' liking of it. Part of me has always wanted to be like him. He has the ability to say what he thinks and not worry about the consequences. I filter so much in my head. I will think a lot about what I'm going to say and then normally decide not to. If I do say something, I really worry afterward; the next day I'll be thinking, 'Jesus, what did I say...?' He's completely the opposite, he says something outrageous and then five minutes later he can't remember he's done it. He's moving on to the next thing. It was a relief to be with someone like that sometimes, because you followed in the slipstream of his confidence.

We had a lot of fun playing together. Being in the most successful England team in decades gave us a little bit more licence to enjoy ourselves. We certainly had a lot of fun batting together in the fleeting moments we did. I was at the crease with him when he got his highest score, his 85 at the Centurion in 2009. I hit my first-ever six as a professional cricketer (*see* page 60). He was just as buzzing as I was. He was laughing and I was never sure whether it was at, or with, me. That never taking anything too seriously was one of his strengths. A bit of it would bounce off him and you'd get into the rhythm of how he went about life. It eased me up. I suddenly had the attitude of, 'Oh, well, we're just messing around here anyway.' It was liberating. Having said that, the *laissez-faire* attitude wasn't unconditional. You wouldn't want to drop a catch. I once dropped AB de Villiers off Swanny's bowling in a test match. It might have been one of the simplest catches I've ever had hit at me. I tried to avoid him for half an hour on the field after that. AB got a hundred.

We both really bowled well when we won in Australia in 2010/11 and became the number-one side in the world. There was a unity in the team that understood we didn't necessarily need to be the best of friends, but could depend on one another on the field. That was different with Swanny and me. We spent a lot of time together off the field too. Almost all our time, in fact. During that brilliant tour, we were afforded the opportunity to do it with some purpose through the vehicle of *Swanny's Diary*, a seven-part tour diary of the Ashes that we posted on YouTube. I'm not sure, had we been losing, that it would have met such widespread approval, but given that we were on this seemingly unstoppable rout, we were allowed some real licence with the comic aspect.

We'd spend our entire coach journeys to the ground, scripting scenes. There were opening gambits where Swanny, the Adelaide Oval in the background, would be caught unaware on the phone talking to his doctor: 'Right, OK, so take two daily? Smear the cream all over the affected area? Should clear up by Tuesday? Thanks, doc.' He would add a comment on the test just gone – for example on Cooky's unbelievable knock in the first test, when he made 235 not out in the second innings: 'It's not every day that a man who runs like Woody from *Toy Story* goes out and scores runs.' We'd script him telling viewers that 'people said we were unusually close when he didn't think that was necessarily the case', as I'd come out of the shower with towels round my head and waist asking if he'd used all of our conditioner. I'd be filming our Christmas-day lunch at the non-families table, everyone looking glum and Swanny saying, 'Tell us another joke, Monty' to Monty Panesar, who'd just shrug.

At one point in the tour, the Aussie media, trying to find anything to dent our momentum, cut an interview to make it seem as if Swanny was mocking their spinner Michael Beer (which he wasn't). So we did our own continuity pieces that would suddenly cut to me massaging Swanny while he was mid-sentence to prove how easy it was to do that sort of editing . We genuinely were beginning to think that, after cricket, the best job in the world must be comic screen writing. That was a real moment in time, a totally unforgettable period in our lives when it felt as if anything was achievable.

Swanny got me out on a rare occasion when we were pitted against each other: a county game between Lancashire and Notts before the test matches began one summer. Bowled first ball. I was really ill. It didn't even spin. I'd have hit it if I hadn't been sick.

Right to Reply: Swanny on Jimmy

He'll claim he had the flu. Don't let him. He'll say, 'It was the first game of the season, it was bitterly cold.' Ridiculous.

I'd hit a lovely four off him when Notts were batting. On the up through the covers. He'd bowled me next ball, then not even bothered celebrating, like he was making a point of how easy it was. Subsequently, when Jimmy came out to bat, Stuart Broad was at mid-off and he said, 'Swanny, I'm not joking, you've got one ball. Imagine the rest of the season.'

I cleaned him up. He played for a bit of turn, it didn't and it went straight through the gate, bowling him middle stump. First ball. Me and Broady were the happiest people in the world. There was one man and his dog watching it at Old Trafford, but we were in a state of pure elation. Someone took a picture with an old-fashioned camera and I had it on my locker for all the tests that summer. Jimmy being cleaned up by me, and Broady beaming back. He wasn't happy about that. He wasn't ill that day either.

As for the De Villiers drop – f**king Jimmy. He's one of the greatest fielders I've ever seen, particularly for a fast bowler. Incredible. But when he's bowling at the other end, he's rubbish. He doesn't concentrate. Drops everything. Earlier in the game someone had edged one off Jimmy to slip. It had landed in front of me and I'd leapt out of the way so it didn't hit my shin. The ball went for four. It didn't look great, to be honest, and Jimmy didn't take to this act of self-preservation very kindly. To be blunt, he went absolutely mad. So, as he tended to, he was still seething about this (and everything else) when I was bowling at the South African middle order later in the day. AB de Villiers, possibly the world's greatest batsman at the time, was in. You needed to get him out, otherwise he would take the game away from you very quickly. He spooned one I bowled very gently into the air. AB never did that. Straight to Jimmy. Inexplicably, it went through his hands. It was one of those that no one in the ground even went 'ooooh', because it was so easy it can't have been a chance. I was in total disbelief looking at him. He shunned the eye contact. I timed my run mid-overs to confront him about it ten minutes later. I said, 'Are you not going to apologize for that?' He said, 'We're even now', as if he'd done it on purpose to annoy me. He hadn't, he was just embarrassed he'd dropped the world's simplest catch. He's so stubborn like that.

I've sat in cars with Jimmy in the morning on the way to cricket grounds genuinely thinking to myself, 'How is anybody married to this man? This is the most miserable man in sport.' He'd sit there in the passenger seat with a scowl on his face for no apparent reason. At first I'd challenge him, wind him up, try to cheer him up, sing in his face, anything, until I started to work out the pattern of the day. You had to wait for his latte to kick in. It was crazy, you could time it to the minute: like magic, the smile would come back and we'd be laughing our way to the ground. Then he would suddenly be very patient. He certainly was with how superstitious I was. (He keeps quiet about it, but I think he is, too.) One day we were driving to Lord's and there was a diversion, which took us all the way through Euston and Camden to get to the ground, all the roads were closed. Then I got four or five wickets. The next day I said, 'Mate, we need to do the same route.' It should have been a ten-minute drive. It took us an hour and a half. I timed telling him until the latte had kicked in. He'd happily sit there like 'Yeah, all right, no worries.'

He'd do that for me – we could listen to our longer playlists. I appreciated it. In fact, when I finished playing, one of the things I asked him was, 'Who do you go to the ground with now?' He told me, 'Broady. He's a more sensible driver than you. It doesn't feel the same yet, but we're working on it.' It was like hearing, 'I've got a new boyfriend. You're still the love of my life but you know, times change, we knew this'd happen, we have to be strong.' I think they've got the hang of it now.

We were like brothers. The only time we fell out, we were in India. I was having a great time on pitches that really suited me. Jimmy wasn't having as much luck. I don't know if that had anything to do with it, because it wasn't cricket-related, but we were hotel-bound. In India, for security reasons, you are never allowed to go out, so we ended up eating all the downtime playing FIFA. Tim Bresnan was winding Jimmy up a treat – he had a special talent for that. The Yorkshireman/Lancastrian thing was always there. Bres scored a screamer and he was all in Jimmy's face. Jimmy wasn't happy. He doesn't like losing. He *really* doesn't like it. I think I laughed or said something to Jimmy like 'All right, mate, calm down.' He didn't speak to me for two days. It genuinely wound him up. I'd be on the bus going, 'Are you really doing this? Are you ignoring me because of FIFA?' That competitive thing is a difficult switch to turn off.

Jimmy and I were probably very similar in our relationships with captains. They knew to trust us when we were bowling and at least let us *think* that we were in control. I'd known Andrew Strauss, who was captain from 2009 to 2012, for a while. He trusted me implicitly when I bowled. He gave me the impression he did, anyway. The only time he didn't was in Melbourne in 2010. I kept beating Michael Clarke's outside edge, but just couldn't take his wicket. Straussy came up to me and, in his public-school tones, said, 'Graeme, how about going round the wicket to the right-hander and having a second slip?' I went, 'Straussy, I don't have anyone caught at second slip.' He said, seemingly getting posher, 'OK, Graeme, let's think about this another way – how often do you post a second slip?' I conceded, 'Oh, yeah, good point.'

He went to second slip. The very next ball Clarke edged it straight to him. I was like 'you absolute hero…' He was bellowing, 'You're a buffoon, Swann', almost fake-evil laughing. It was that kind of delicate balancing act.

It could have been tricky with Cooky when he became captain because he and I had been friends and Jimmy and I both definitely had the potential to rebuff being told what to do. Cooky knew what made us work, though, which was letting us have our own way. He'd suggest an idea, I'd tell him to get stuffed and then three balls later I'd suddenly say, 'Oh, let's give that a try', but make it look like it was my idea. Jimmy's pretty much the same. If you tell Jimmy to do something, you're on a hiding to nothing. If you kind of plant the seed, he might come around. It's one of the reasons Jimmy is the best bowler we've ever had. He doesn't ever listen to anyone else. If they're saying, 'He's beating the guy too often without taking his wicket, he needs to bowl his variation.' He knows that the reason his record is better than anyone's is that he plays the longest, most patient waiting game for a fast bowler that there's ever been. Then when he does eventually bowl the variation, the batsman is almost thinking, 'He can't do it', so it's a surprise. Jimmy Anderson is the best I've ever seen. Not just because of the delivery of his skills, but because of the thought process behind it.

He'd have been a brilliant general.

He'd make an even better coach. Jimmy would take practice seriously. I was more of the belief that it was quality over quantity. Maybe that was inherent laziness. If I bowled 10 or 15 balls, and it felt right, that would be enough for me. Whereas Jimmy would have a proper bowl. But he never stopped working on new things. He bowls the most perfect wobble-seam ball now – I reckon it's got him 100 test wickets. I remember that idea coming to him. He was watching Stuart Clark bowl for Australia, studying this new thing he was doing that he hadn't seen before. He asked David Saker, 'Is that on purpose?' David, the fount of fast-bowling knowledge, recognized it as the-seam ball and showed him. Jimmy mastered it the first time he tried it. The important thing, though, was that, rather than thinking, 'That's in my locker' and moving on, he'd practise it religiously. Every young bowler who came in, he'd be very happy to show them, too; he'd take them aside and tell them, 'This is how you bowl this.' It's this kind of openness, dedication to learning and evergreen curiosity that makes him the bowler he is. Couple that with the fact that he's so moody on the field, getting stuck into batsmen so much, that he makes them forget what he's doing with the ball and distracts them into a personal battle with him. That's part of the genius. They stop thinking all the important things like 'How's he trying to set me up?' and get emotionally involved instead. They stop being analytical. He's the cleverest bowler I've ever known.

Working on *Swanny's Diary* was the dream, being comic TV writers in Australia while winning the Ashes. Jimmy plays the comedian's straight man so well it's ridiculous. We were given free rein. We capitalized on the fact that no one really understood the potential of social media at the time. They saw it as, 'Oh, we'll let them do it.' They wouldn't let us now. We probably ruined it for every England team to come after, because we took it too far. As Hugh Morris, who was our managing director at the time, once said about Twitter and cricketers, 'It's like giving monkeys machine guns.' Back then, I don't think anyone even approved it. We just did it and posted it.

I used to love bowling with Jimmy. I often wonder if he thinks of himself like I did, mumbling to myself, 'They'll miss me when I'm gone', while I was toiling all day from an end. The greatest legacy of mine was that people realized how good I was once I'd gone. Like a painter who's destitute, living on the streets while he paints, but then once he's died, the family are cashing in.

Seriously, I love everything about Jimmy. The thing people often misinterpret is that what seems like moodiness is more often down to shyness. In social situations we dovetail quite nicely because I'm the exact opposite: I dive in, talk to everyone, become the overbearing idiot. I'm more comfortable with that. I'm like a puppy and he's like a kitten. I love everyone straight away, licking their faces and all sorts. You need to win Jimmy's trust before he'll come and sit on your lap.

My fondest memories are of when we had bowled a team out. That's when bowlers are happiest. You'll never see people happier in your life than a successful bowling side that has just got back into the dressing room. My abiding memory of Jimmy is that before you knew it, straight away, he'd have his shorts on and be getting the crosswords out. It'd be like, 'Right, let's get on with the real business.' We'd be going through the papers, just like mates messing around, without a care. It was lovely. I miss that. I'd say it's unbelievable he's still playing, but it's not. I always thought he would outlast us all.

JIMMY AND SWANNY'S DRIVING TO THE GAME PLAYLIST

Hurts – *Better Than Love*
Biffy Clyro – *Black Chandelier*
Everything Everything – *Cough Cough*
Matchbox Twenty – *3am*
The Maccabees – *Went Away*
Bastille – *Pompeii*
Kasabian – *Switchblade Smiles*
Wild Beasts – *We Still Got the Taste Dancin' on Our Tongues*
White Lies – *Farewell to the Fairground*
Wham! – *Young Guns (Go For It)*
Semisonic – *Closing Time*
Black Box – *Ride On Time**

*Swanny's *pièce de résistance*

Stuart Broad

126 tests and counting...

437 wickets @ 29.1

3064 runs @ 19.3

Of all the dressing rooms in all the grounds in all the world, he walks into mine.

How can I forget the first time we met?

That flowing blonde hair.

Striking blue eyes

That perfect figure.

I thought, 'My God ... she's beautiful.'

It's terrifying and very surreal that we have become the second oldest opening partnership in test history in terms of our ages. Curtly Ambrose and Courtney Walsh were still bowling together when they were 36 and 37. We'll be 37 and 33. A combined age of 70. A thousand test wickets between us. That's a lot of bowling we've done together.

People say, 'Can you believe it's 11 years?'

I can. It feels like longer sometimes.

The beginning of the partnership was a surprise selection in Wellington, New Zealand, in 2008. The team was struggling out there, with myself and Broady watching from the sidelines. The then coach Peter Moores made the brave call of bringing us in for Steve Harmison and Matthew Hoggard. They were real old-guard, untouchable cricketers, who rightly had their names carved into English cricket history as greats of the game after their heroic Ashes performances two years previously. I'm not sure if we were conscious at the time that it was such a dramatic 'changing of the guard', but it was certainly quite a shock for everyone. Understandably, we both felt a lot of pressure replacing those two. The teams were read out the day before. Harmy bowled the speed of lightning in the nets out of anger. We were slightly embarrassed, treading on eggshells around them. I think it was probably worse for Stuart than for me because he had never played with them at all, so in his eyes they were these cricketers he'd only ever seen on television, not people he'd have dreamed of playing instead of. It was slightly sacrilege. But we will both always have a lot to be grateful for, for the confidence that Peter Moores instilled in us with that decision. It was one of those test matches where everything came together. It could have easily gone the other way.

We batted first, so I didn't take part in the first day at all. I felt all pent up just watching. I was desperate, as always, to be involved. For a bowler who bats low down the order, it's like being back in the classroom sometimes when you bat first – you're just staring out of the window, wishing you were there. In those days, we'd play football at the end of the day. I think I might have been a bit over-tenacious given the circumstances, let loose in a kickabout having been kicking around the dressing room all day. Pulling the strings in the middle of the pitch, I tried to do a Cruyff turn unchallenged. I twisted my ankle. Everyone stood there confused, having just seen me tackle myself after sitting doing nothing all day, while I rolled around on the floor. I left the ground on crutches. Luckily the media had all left by then, but as I was walking out of the ground I bumped into Gus Fraser – former England fast bowler, then working as a journalist – a cosmic coincidence given his fast-bowling heritage. He looked at me, sighed and said, 'What the bloody hell have you done?'

I iced it all night. When I woke up it was totally swollen and really painful. Thankfully that morning we were still batting. When I went out to bat myself, it was agony. Trying to run was sheer pain. I remember being worried for the team, because it was going to upset the balance, worried for myself, because this was a huge opportunity, but at the forefront of my mind was the worry that, if this ruled me out, football would be banned. I'd be public enemy number one in the dressing room. I've now been in the team long enough to remember football being banned twice. It's a saving grace that it's never been my fault. Thankfully, during that test, I was able just to run through the pain and the more I ran on it, the better it got. The pitch swung, which made it bit easier. I ended up taking 5-for and Broady picked up three wickets overall. We won the test. We were both so delighted we had done well. It was an amazing moment.

There had been similar circumstances the first time we ever played together, in that I was stubbornly playing through an injury that, in truth, I would have been advised not to. It was in a one-day international at the 2007 World Cup. I broke my finger. He got called up into the squad as a last minute replacement for me, but while he was on the plane on his way over, I decided to stay out. We chased down 300 against West Indies in Barbados. I thought, how many more World Cups am I going to play in? Does it matter if I don't get a rod in it and it's not 100 per cent straight for the rest of my life? Not really. Me and Stuart won the game with the bat at the end. The unlikeliest of heroes.

We've been lucky in a lot of ways, in that we've never been in competition as bowlers. We've always been different enough in our skills that we haven't been a direct threat to each other's places. Stuart has been under pressure at times from the bowlers who get steep bounce and move the ball off the seam and I have from the skiddier ones who swing the ball. It's never been me or him in selections. So, we've had a nice balance. Part of our evolution as a partnership has been about talking all the time. You hear about a lot of fast bowlers trying to out-bowl each other, but we've always had the attitude that fast bowling is something you do in partnerships. The conversation has really helped us. 'Shall I try this?' 'No, stick to the plan' – we'll be checking each other all the time. As we've grown, we've been able to find our own little tricks and reference points that keep us in a good zone. Stuart found that, when he was walking back to his mark, it was useful for him to look above the stand, taking himself out of the ground for a minute. It was almost as if the perspective calmed him down and helped him find his instinctive rhythm. It's not something that works for me, but I have a similar idea in that I try to keep a song in my head. You're just giving yourself a break from being too tense or conscious.

As a new-ball partnership, the trick is always to assess the conditions more quickly than the opening batsmen. You have to think on your feet and notice the pitch's strengths and weaknesses before they do. It's like a little mind game of sussing each other out. As well as the conspiring, there has been a lot of consoling. The slips will have dropped another catch and I'll be calming him down. There'll be plenty of moaning about batters, one of us saying, 'How can they not score runs on this pitch?' while the other rolls his eyes before running in. There's a confidentiality pact between us.

We can't always keep each other in check, though. I've sat in many a post-match disciplinary room with Stuart. I've watched him, partly in awe, as he is shown his dissent back by the official. He, without exception, will be looking back at them and saying, 'Yeah. But it's out, though.' The game will be done. Everyone will have gone home. The decision will be not out. He's being fined for his reaction. And he still wants it reviewed. You've got to respect that.

One thing that has made partnering Stuart Broad over the years never get long in the tooth is his ability to produce moments of brilliance from nowhere. He's always had that capability to change a game in a really short spell. He's won the most vital games of a generation with inspired short bursts of bowling. I remember missing out with an injury when he bowled out Australia in the Ashes in 2015. He took his 300th test wicket in his first over and finished with 8-15. Their scorecard fitted on a tweet. Trent Bridge was in a genuine state of shock. Not least him, who was pictured all over the front of every newspaper the next day with his hands over his mouth, face frozen in disbelief at Stokes' diving catch off him to dismiss Adam Voges. He looked like a little boy who had just been given the best birthday present ever. It was a pretty transcendent moment, a very rare and totally unguarded reaction. I think it connected because it was how everyone would hope what playing for their country would feel like. I was very jealous of him getting to bowl on that surface.

Further back, there was the spell at the Oval that won us the Ashes in 2009. He just tore through the Australians without any warning and ended the first innings with 5-37. It was series-defining. He's always had that, a magic tendency simmering somewhere, but these days he can sense when it's happening, too. He'll say, 'I feel really good here, one wicket and it might set me off.' I've never had it. Give me the ball, I'm feeling good? Nah.

Even within a conscientious unit of fast bowling, there are still some personal politics. How could there not be? I know he occasionally thinks he gets a rough deal with getting second pick on the end he bowls. He's developed this tactic that he doesn't realize I've cottoned on to, trying to double-bluff me when we turn up at a ground. He'll ask what end I want. I'll go, 'I'm not sure yet' and he'll say, 'Nah, that'll definitely suit you that end, the wind and the slope and that.' I know he'll say he gets second pick, but I wouldn't let him get the violins out on that one, he gets his say plenty.

Of course, given the length of time we've spent with each other, I've witnessed some really difficult moments for him, too. Yuvraj Singh hit him for six sixes in the T20 World Cup in India in 2007. A couple went over my head. Miles over my head. That was quite a steep learning curve for him. He also got hit in the face by a bouncer that freakishly went through his grill: that was against India at Old Trafford in 2014. I remember him coming back to the dressing room in slight shock, pretty composed, but with blood everywhere. It sparked him having dreams where he imagined cricket balls flying at him, waking up bolt upright in bed. I empathized, because I have those all the time. I think most cricketers do. My most common one is that I'll be walking down the street and a ball will come flying at me out of nowhere. Or I'll bowl, and the ball gets hit back at me seriously hard. I always wake up when it is inches from my nose. Those dreams are common for all of us.

I really respected the way Stuart responded to being left out in the West Indies in 2019. We played in Sri Lanka with three spinners and he would have expected to be left out, but in the Windies a month later he was dropped in favour of a similar player in Sam Curran. Stuart was incredible. He just got on with it. It was really telling as to how he's made himself the bowler he is. He trained really hard, practised really hard, mucked in. I can remember being left out of teams and I wish I'd reacted the way he did. I had a lot of respect for that. A common initial misconception of Stuart in the early days was that he was a bit of a show pony. He's not. He works so hard. He got back in the side and showed how valuable he was to us. To do that without sulking is a rare trait.

We get the same car to grounds now. He's not got the same music taste as Swanny and me. He'll hear the first bars of Oasis's 'Cigarettes and Alcohol' and ask, in all sincerity, 'What's this?' I despair of that. The playlist sharing isn't the same with him. But we have a vital shared interest. Everyone else wants to get in early to get into the nets and start practising. Me and Broady would rather have another half-hour in bed. We try to get there at the last possible moment.

He likes to bang on about the fast bowlers' union, about looking out for each other's backs and not bowling short at each other in the nets or games, but the last time I played against him, he bowled me a bouncer. It was right at my neck. It got me out fending. I thought that was very interesting (if you want to refresh your memory, turn back to page 17 for a more complete rundown of this brutal episode).

Right to Reply: Broady on Jimmy

Well, yes. There is some truth in that. Jimmy and I *do* have a sort of honourable agreement that we don't bounce each other. Our lives are hard enough as it is. There were extenuating circumstances here, though. Jimmy had come to the crease. I'd stayed respectful to our covenant, pitching it up for about 15 balls. He was doing the right thing his end, too, leaving the ball outside off stump, giving the pitch a tap, leaving the ball. I think he liked the idea that he was setting himself up to go big. Jimmy always bats as if that's a genuine possibility. Either way, for a while our little mutual agreement was being respected by all parties. Another fast bowler, and by default a member of the union, Graham Onions, was at the other end. I know Bunny, as we call him, really well. He's a really nice guy. I pitched it up at him, too. It was the morally right thing to do. I thought I heard him nick the ball to the keeper and appealed. Out of nothing, as they'd crossed for a single for byes, he had a pop at me. I can't remember exactly what he said, probably because I was mid-red-misting (that's a thing for us fast bowlers), but it was something along the lines of 'You know I've not hit that. If you need to cheat your way to wickets, that's your game.' As I absorbed it in slight disbelief, I thought to myself, there is no way I'm having that. I built myself into a bit of a grump on the way back to my mark. By the time I'd reached it, I was full-blown red mist. The problem was, Jimmy was on strike now, not Bunny. I bounced him and he gloved it to slip. He can blame Graham Onions for that.

Don't let Jimmy make you feel like he's been hard done by, though. The thing you have to learn pretty quickly is, even if you've spent an entire career playing with him and, like me, consider him a genuinely close friend, as soon as you play *against* him, I wouldn't bother trying to say hello on the field. It's like you've suddenly become an Australian. You'll find yourself scratching your head, mining your memory of the past week and thinking, 'Did I say something out of turn the other day when he was round for a glass of red? Nothing seemed up at the time.'

The first time I played against him was for Leicestershire in 2005. I was a little bit star-struck because it was only two years earlier that I'd been in the crowd at Lord's, watching him open the bowling against South Africa. On this occasion, Lancashire were chasing a target towards the end and he actually got a few runs. They got so close. They needed two to win and he got out. We won by one run. I remember, even from across the pitch, noticing how distraught he was. It was the slowest walk off a pitch I'd ever seen. Like I say, that's the thing with Jimmy. I've seen him get out a thousand times. We all have. But it's as if it's a genuine shock to him every time. I know people call him the Burnley Lara, but sometimes I wonder if he thinks he's actually Brian Lara. The rest of us are watching him not knowing whether he's left- or right-handed. Even in Sydney in 2017/18, we'd had a poor tour and Australia were about to make it 4-0 conclusively with a day and a half to spare. Jimmy was given out caught behind, the last wicket to fall. He was disconsolate, pleading with the umpire that he hadn't hit it. Everyone in the ground was thinking, 'Thank God this is over, we can go home', apart from Jimmy. He wanted to carry on batting. I admire that about him really. He's the most competitive bloke you'll ever meet.

Our first test tour together was at the end of 2007 in Sri Lanka.

Swanny, Jimmy and I were all in the squad, but on the outskirts of the team. When you're twelfth man, a job we were essentially sharing for the whole tour, you spend eight hours a day getting the drinks ready for the breaks and running back and forth onto the pitch. It's quite a full-on job and can be quite laborious if you don't make your own fun. So, accidentally, it was an opportunity for us to get to know each other. It was a good thing we did because I'm not sure any of us knew all the things we were going to go through together in the subsequent years. The thing you don't necessarily realize with Jimmy is that he is quite shy. Before you get to know him, you think, 'He doesn't give you a lot', but as soon as you break that down, he's a really funny and warm character. That Sri Lanka tour was my opportunity to do that. By the time we got in the team together, he felt like a friend rather than a grumpy Burnley man.

People tend to remember us both being included in the Wellington test as the opening pair in 2008, but actually, the first-ever game we played together was Brian Lara's last-ever game in Barbados. Ironically, Jimmy was the hero with the bat in Barbados. He came out to bat nine down with four or five to win. We knocked off the winning runs. It's funny, given that we've taken 1,000 test wickets collectively, that our first experience together on a cricket field was with the bat. You'd never have thought that our first bit of magic, if you can call it that, was scrambling to a win with the bat in the Windies.

One of the really telling things about Jimmy and me ever since then, though, is that we've never felt as if we were in competition with each other. I know that sounds like a weird thing to say. It's definitely not common practice. Before I became an England player

I'd heard all these stories of Andy Caddick and Darren Gough being constantly desperate to outdo each other. Not celebrating each other's wickets and so on. Maybe because Peter Moores gave us our chance together, telling us that we were going to be the two who would push the bowling attack forward, it's almost always felt as if he and I have had the responsibility together. We won that test together and have spent our careers in parallel from that moment on. It's come quite naturally. We're both very competitive, but in a team-orientated way. We don't care if Jimmy gets 8-for or I get 8-for. Because actually, in the cold light of day, the quicker we get ten wickets, the quicker we're drinking tea and watching us bat. Why would you ever want to be stood up in the field when you can be sat down in the changing room? That's been our attitude. One of the few pay-offs of being a fast bowler is that, when you do your job well, you get to sit down sooner. No further incentive required. As much as Jimmy loves bowling, I don't think he loves anything more than doing the crossword with his feet up.

Not ever feeling that we are in direct competition, though, doesn't mean that we haven't fallen out occasionally. There's one moment I remember very well during the second innings of an Ashes test against Australia in 2013. They were chasing 300 or so and it was beginning to derail for us. Jimmy had a couple that were run away to fine leg or sliced away. Shane Watson was clipping him off his legs for four. There were a couple of misfields, one through Cooky's hands for four. It was like a goldrush in a game of bingo for things that annoy fast bowlers. Remember the red mist? Jimmy had started to see it. He was shouting at everyone, cursing the ground and it was making everyone seize up a little bit. Cooky, who hadn't been captain very long, came up to me and said, 'Can you have a word with Jimmy? We don't want this to go through the group.' I thought to myself, Jesus Christ, talk about drawing the short straw. I spent an over or two observing this very angry man from Burnley seething to himself and trying to work out exactly how it was possible to go and tell him to, in Cooky's words, 'stop behaving like a nob'. I couldn't for the life of me imagine a situation where that would go down well.

I took my chance mid-over when we crossed paths. I went up to him. 'Jimmy. Ummm. Jimmy. Errr. Have a little think about your body language here.' He's staring back at me through the red mist as I continue, 'Because, you look a bit angry and a bit stressed and are having a go at everyone a little bit.'

He heard what I had to say and without flinching told me, in no uncertain terms, where to go.

It was in the general region of what I had imagined the response might be. Trying to get the conversation in before the next ball was bowled, I continued, slightly emboldened, potentially red-misting myself, 'I'm only passing a message on for the team here and you're behaving like a nob.'

He didn't like that either. 'Did you not hear me? I've told you to f**k off.'

We ended up just rallying expletives back at each other. There were 40 minutes until tea. We didn't speak for the entirety, bowling at either end, both wound up. To his eternal credit, during tea, the game in the balance, he found me while I was still keeping my distance and said, 'You were dead right there, I was behaving like an idiot. Thank you. Red mist.' He got 10-for and won us the game.

It was one of the best tests I'd ever been involved in. That built our relationship massively. We suddenly knew that we could always have a blow out and it would actually do us good. There's something of a proper friendship in that. We knew we could speak our minds to each other without jeopardizing too much.

It's not something I've ever worried about, because it's been a constant source of inspiration and evolution bowling with Jimmy, but however senior I get opening the bowling, he'll always get first dibs on which end he wants to bowl. It's something I've learned to accept. He's the chairman of selectors in that regard, he'll get the final say. We know it's usually the most beneficial thing for the team that he bowls at the end that suits his away-swing better. So that will usually be the deciding factor. Fortunately, quite often we prefer different ends anyway. I've learned to, at first begrudgingly, love the ends I bowl from. You make them your own through familiarity. The Oval and Trent Bridge are like that. Headingley is an interesting one, though. We were very stubborn on the ends we bowled from for seven or eight years. I'd always bowl up the hill (obviously) and he would bowl down it. After doing this for nearly a decade, we just looked at each other and said, 'Look, we're crap every time we come here, let's try swapping ends.' He got 10-for. Problem solved.

I have learned to be able to sense when I'm feeling good and something might happen. It used to just explode out of me beyond my control almost, or I'd be really confused that it hadn't. But as well as being able to read my own intuition, I've really tried to learn consistency from Jimmy. On the days when Jimmy feels crap, he is still able to get 3-40 from 25 overs, whereas I'll get 0-60. I've seen him feel out of rhythm and bowl 13- or 14-over spells. He's got the heart of a lion. It's like the adage you hear about football teams that win the league – the champions get results when they play badly. Jimmy has this unique blend of natural talent and control with the ball, physical and mental steel, but also the ability to not let anything external affect him when he's in the moment. That's a skill in itself. Sport is such a strange industry to work in because people expect you to be a robot. They would never allow for the fact that an argument you may have had in the morning away from the game might affect you later in the day. Maybe you've got 50 e-mails and people chasing you that are making you really stressed. There are so many little things that can eat away at you and take away from what you are trying to achieve. Jimmy has not let anything distract him from what's happening on a cricket field when it's happening. That's an art in itself for a bloke who's got two kids and a family he has to spend a lot of time away from and so on.

If there's another thing I'm grateful for having Jimmy for over all these years, it's that someone knows what you're going through. I've lost count of the number of times we've been 30-3 and Jimmy and I have had this little look at each other. A little glance that just says, 'Uh oh, here we go.' You're feeling each other's pain. It's why we have bowlers' unions – at Nottinghamshire we call ourselves the cartel. In those moments, you have to make each other happy. You start comforting each other ahead of the inevitable workload that you thought you were going to be spared for a while. It suddenly becomes a bit like 'Come on, I'll make you a coffee.' We've had our moans together at the batting group. Let's not for one second think that the batters haven't had a moan at us getting wickets. When it gets a bit flat, the batters have been bounced out by 95 miles an hour and short leg is going, 'God, we're rubbish, why can't we bowl bouncers at them?' If I'd had the skill to bowl like Graeme Swann, that would have been the dream. Bowl off-spin like a genius, field at second slip and catch everything and have an ability with the bat where, if you get caught at cover, people can just say, 'That's the way he plays.' I don't hurt too badly any more in the mornings. I used to hurt more when I was 21 or 22. My body has almost become immune to it now.

One thing I'd say about fast bowling to anyone who wants to do it is that the feeling you get from getting a batsman out with a plan, or bowling at someone who's hopping around or they nick one to the slips and get caught…the emotion for 15 seconds after you make that breakthrough is like no other. You're putting in such physical effort, such mental application, and you can literally break open a game for your team, ten other men or women, in one moment, with a skill… It's very hard to replicate that feeling. You can literally hold the ball and, if you don't move, the game can't go anywhere. If you bowl a jaffa, an unplayable delivery, you can get the best batsman in the world out. You can take 0-100 on the first day, drop back in on the second day, get 5-20 and win the Ashes. It is an amazing game like that sometimes.

Cricketers are the sort of friends where you have spent so much time together, you can go without seeing each other for six weeks, bump into each other and have the best night. Swanny, Cooky, Matt Prior, Jimmy. Especially given everything we've been through. You can fall back into that changing-room atmosphere immediately and relax. I'm sure he'll be a great mate for life.

Alastair Cook

It's testament to the amount of time I have spent with Cooky that this book is filled with stories that either refer back to him or are about him. Scarily enough, we have spent pretty much our entire young-adult lives together. In hotel rooms. On planes. In the middle. On buses. In the nets. While the personnel in England teams has changed regularly, thankfully for me there was always a constant. Alastair Cook. I don't think there'll be another English batsman like him. Certainly not one who is as successful for such a long period of time. If anyone ever comes close, I can tell you one thing for sure. They won't be an ex-chorister, flute-playing farmer. I've had to get used to phrases like 'lambing season' in the dressing room over the years. It wasn't something we had a lot of in Burnley. Some people might think that the farming stuff is slightly elaborated for narrative ends, but he actually is a proper, real-life farmer. He certainly knows his way around a sheep.

The cultural difference between us, though bridged throughout our career, was most striking the first time we came across each other. I remember it clearly to this day. Lancashire vs Essex. The entire Lancastrian side, some of them pretty mild-mannered, really laid into Cooky when he came out to bat. He'd just got a double hundred against Australia in the warm-ups for the soon-to-be-infamous 2005 Ashes. For some reason, we all assumed he must be really arrogant. This was before he gathered a reputation as the most decent, even-mannered man in cricket. It was just taken as a given that if he was that good, there had to be something wrong with him as a bloke. The battle plan, though I'm not sure we had really premeditated it, was to let him know what we thought of him. I got him out. I'd love to say that it was a great ball that he nicked, but it was a long hop. Maybe the tactic of having a go at him worked that day. Later, once fielding sides had got to know Cooky's temperament, they hardly ever used it on him. There would be no point even engaging in it. He would give absolutely nothing back. He didn't that day, even if I did decide that the best mode of welcome was with some 'direct' language. When he was in one of his runs of form, of which there were many, he'd just be stood there, marking his guard in typically gawkish fashion, totally sweat free (he has a strange, slightly poetic biological make-up that means he never sweats), with all the time in the world and not a false shot, while bowlers toiled and screamed and scratched and hoped. It must have been maddening. I'm glad I didn't bowl at him competitively too often after that day.

I flew out with him from an England A tour in the West Indies to the seniors in India not long after our county introduction. It was two days of constant travelling to join the Test team. Having not really spoken since our meeting on the pitch, I think he was slightly concerned that I might behave the same way off the field as I had on it and that he was in for a long 48 hours. We were sat next to each other, about to take off for the first of many flights, and he just turned to me and said 'The last time we spoke you called me a c**t'. I knew from that moment, that we were going to be fine. He scored a hundred on test debut. For the next 12 years, that was me. Sleeping in the dressing room while he batted. Glaring at him when he dropped something off me at slip. Being asked by him if 'there was any chance I could pitch it up a bit' behind half-grimaced, half-gritted teeth. Despite our opposite disciplines, him the southern opening bat, me the northern opening bowler, we became very close over the time together. So much so that he's godfather to my eldest, Lola, and our family get down to the farm when we can in off season. In his house, he has replaced parts of his banister with stumps he's collected from landmark tests. My interest was piqued by that, as I have been wondering of late what to do with the various balls and stumps I've collected myself over the years. I have two pictures of me with the Queen by the bathroom, but other than that nothing is on display. Having inspected his innovation, I won't be dismantling my banister any time soon.

The brusque nature of our meeting at Lancashire, which to be honest had been entirely my doing, did in fact stand us in good stead for our subsequent relationship. We knew that we could say anything to each other and it wouldn't be the end of the world. That's a precious foundation to have with someone when navigating the many extremes of test cricket, especially between a strike bowler and a captain, which we evolved into. I knew that he wasn't afraid to tell me what he thought and that I could disagree; we could have a little blow out, then would come back round. We both wanted the same thing: to win games of cricket for England. I don't know whether it was conscious or otherwise, but I felt as if he knew the exact mindset I needed to be in to bowl. Right on that cusp between focus and the red mist.

Of course, you can't always get the balance right.

He dropped me once for a one-day game. I'd been rested for a series and Bres had come in for me and bowled really well. They decided, when I returned, that Bres would keep his place. I wasn't happy about that at all. He didn't keep me on the cusp between focus and red mist in the meeting when he broke the news. My exact language would probably need to be highly edited in any form of published work, but if I remember correctly, it was along the lines of 'You're out of order, mate.' I couldn't tell you verbatim, though. I left the room with a little storm cloud over my head like Charlie Brown. The complexity with the ensuing few days was not only were we both very stubborn and not prepared to back down on this one, but also, given that we'd become close friends and had our specific spots on buses or plane journeys, we would spend a lot of our time literally next to each other. On the way to the ground, we didn't speak. During the game, nothing. On the way back, nothing. Travelled to the next game, nothing. Then there was an injury on the eve of the game and I ended up playing anyway. Which was slightly awkward given we'd got so worked up about it. I apologized after that and life went back to normal. I like to think that the moral for captains on that one would be, don't rest me. I don't take to it too well.

The end of Cooky's career for England was something I'd known for a while was going to come and, to be honest, dreaded a bit. I'd built up such a deep admiration for the way he had ridden out so many difficult moments in his career to consistently prove and then reprove what a special cricketer he was. He did it all with such grace, too. When the end did come, he told me personally on the balcony at Trent Bridge. A test match before it was officially announced. It was quite surreal hearing the words come out of his mouth, but he had such clarity. From that moment on, I was slightly concerned that when the moment came, it was going to be a bit emotional for me.

When we reached the Oval, it had been an exhausting-to-play, exhilarating-to-watch (so I'm told) summer; the series against India that had felt constantly in the balance still was. More importantly, every cricket fan in England came out to watch Alastair Cook's last test. It was one of the most extraordinary test matches I've ever been involved in. You just knew he was going to get a hundred. There was a feeling like I'd never experienced in a cricket ground. People bunked work and skipped school to get to the fourth day, which was a Monday, because he was not out overnight. You could sense the amount of their lives everyone had invested in being there to watch him. There was this hushed reverence, people desperate to drink in every second of a trademark Cooky test innings for the last time, everyone pouring a goodbye to a part of their own lives through it. The struggles. The calamities. The successes. It was suddenly distinctly in focus what that cumulatively had meant, not just to me and the other players around him, but to the cricketing public. It was very moving when he did it. It was like the longest encore you'll ever see at a concert. The applause didn't feel as if it would ever end. I thought it was the most Cooky thing in the world that, out of mild embarrassment eventually, the whole ground still on its feet, he started marking his guard again. Ready for the next ball. He book-ended his career with hundreds.

I'd love to say I soaked the entire innings in like everyone else, but as I mentioned earlier (*see* page 111) I was asleep for most of it. I guess it wouldn't have been right otherwise. I already miss the moment when I'd see him straight-punch the ball back past the bowler, know that all was right with the world and find a corner of the dressing room to fall asleep in, with the certain knowledge I wouldn't be needed for a while.

The layers of meaning of that particular test match got deeper, too. With India chasing an unlikely victory, I eventually took the last wicket to become the highest wicket-taking fast bowler in the history of the game. It was the last ball of Cooky's career, retiring as the highest run scorer in English test-cricket history by some distance. He was standing where he'd begun all those years before, at slip. It couldn't have been more perfect. I did nearly crack in the post-match interview, narrowly holding it together as I described him as my best mate.

Who knows how many wickets I would have taken by now if he could catch?

CHAPTER 7

Ashes to Ashes

A big pot of constant hysteria/apprehension/

agony/euphoria/repeat...

The Biggest Yet

Since my first Ashes in 2006, I've been involved in every kind of situation an England cricketer can find himself in. Never-ending whitewash humiliations. Era-defining overseas victories. Hanging on by any means necessary with the bat for precious draws. Wildly celebrating nail-biting home wins. The thing you come to realize with the Ashes, once you've played a few, is that every single time you arrive to play in one, it's 'absolutely massive' or 'the biggest yet' or 'the most watched series ever'. The appetite for it doesn't ever seem to fade.

If I search for it in my memory, there's a movie reel of all past series – some small moments as if they were yesterday, others blurred into a big pot of constant hysteria/apprehension/agony/euphoria/repeat. Here are a few of the big ones I've fished out. I've chosen to share more positive moments than otherwise, but rest assured there has been a sizeable catalogue of each over the years. I might have seen everything, but it still hasn't armed me to find any suitable answer to the most frequently asked question in my life:

'We gonna win the Ashes, then?'

I honestly don't know, mate. Hang on, I'll just get my crystal ball out.

Look the Part

Australia vs England
23 November 2006
First Test, Close of Day One
The Gabba, Brisbane
Australia 346-3
J M Anderson 18-4-88-0

England had won at home in 2005, bringing back the Ashes for the first time in 18 years. The whole country, for the first time in my life, was unified in its wholehearted, unflinching focus on the cricket. It was an attention rarely even reserved for football. The greatest series of all time. I watched, with more awe than frustration, but admittedly a little of the latter, as a fan like the rest of the country, while being carted around the country playing county cricket. In a state of flux and regrowth with my bowling, I'd been included in the squad for the last test as a replacement for Simon Jones, who had bowled beautifully but suffered an unfortunate flare-up of a recurring injury problem. With England 2-1 up with one to go, they opted to play Paul Collingwood instead, to balance the side with enough batsmen in case they found themselves in a rear-guard situation for a draw. Draw they did and the Ashes were ours.

The side famously celebrated the next day at Downing Street, atop open-roof buses and behind sunglasses that failed to hide that they'd enjoyed the evening's partying even more than anyone watching might have done. The closest I'd got to the action was at Old Trafford, where I'd gone to see the Lancashire physio for some persistent injury issues and snuck in so I could watch the test. Every seat was taken, so I was perched in the aisle, watching as closely as everybody else. Looking back at that moment, I don't know if I felt I was ever going to play for England in an Ashes again. You never know. I hoped.

Despite missing the entire following summer because of quite a serious stress fracture, I found myself on the plane to Australia for the return series at the end of 2006. It was probably the most indifferent period of my career in terms of my bowling rhythm. I'm not sure if you could even call it rhythm. I had hardly bowled at all. I played one county game right at the end of the season and, with Jones injured again, that was deemed enough for me to be selected for the tour.

This was a seriously big series in Australia. The home team, which still read back-to-back like a list of the all-time greats of the game but with a good few coming close to retirement, were desperate to settle a score as their swan song. The Australian public were suddenly engaged in a different way, having dominated themselves into a kind of smug boredom in recent years. Glenn McGrath, as was his custom, did a press conference saying he expected to win 5-0. I watched it. He always said it. But it wasn't just lip service.

He really meant it. Ricky Ponting was no less forthcoming. Our own captain Michael Vaughan, the architect of the '05 victory, was injured, which left Freddie Flintoff in charge of a side that, unbeknown even to ourselves at the time, was suddenly slightly off-balance.

To me, the biggest alarm bell of the whole thing sounded before we even left. There was a lot of talk from the senior members about 'portraying the right image'. We were prepped on how we needed to look when we got off the plane, suits meticulously planned, looking a million dollars. I never really understood why the suits were such a big deal. There was so much chat about how we were going to look when we turned up. The Manchester City football team turn up to games wearing matching jeans and t-shirts, but it doesn't seem to hinder them too much. They look like a unit and they prioritize their actual job. To be honest, I think that, in the middle of all the soap-opera build-up, some of us had forgotten we were going to play any cricket.

I was picked for the first test and, in searing heat, walked out with the rest of the side for the first day of the Ashes in front of 42,000 people at the Gabba. As we walked, we still had a bit of a 2005 fairy-tale swagger to us. I was standing at mid-on. Steve Harmison, the tormentor of all those big names back in England, had the new ball. It was time for the talking to stop. Everyone was fixated on the first statement of what was supposedly the biggest series down under ever.

Harmy bowled the first ball to second slip.

There was a split second when everyone in the ground stopped, as if thinking to themselves, 'Did I dream that?'

You could feel it. The entire bubble of 2005, all that believing and posturing, just went 'pop'. Harmy laughed it off and Freddie, being the recipient in the slip cordon, got rid of the ball immediately, as if doing so might make it look as if nothing had happened. But it had. The damage, already, was done. I was thinking to myself, 'Brilliant, I've missed the one successful Ashes ever and suddenly we're back in the 1990s all over again.' I don't mean anything against Harmy. He was a hero for England on so many occasions, one of the greatest ever, but being an opening bowler, as I learned farther down the line, is a huge responsibility in setting the tone. You're beginning the story. The first line to this one left the ending almost immediately inevitable.

It was downhill from there. Australia ended day one 346-3. Oof. That's a big body blow on the first day of a series. I went totally wicketless all day. Of course, you do all the chat, to the outside world and to yourselves, that you'll just let it go and move on, but there was no escaping the feeling that we were in for a brutal couple of months. It proved so.

That first test just got worse and worse. Australia amassed 602-9. A pretty ominous opening statement. They won at a canter, by 277 runs. We lost the series 5-0. I took five wickets in the entire series, being moved in and out of the side to help the balance in the batting when Monty Panesar replaced Ashley Giles. It wasn't a very enjoyable experience. I wasn't anywhere near the bowler I am now and it was quite a vulnerable learning curve to be on. It felt as if everybody Australia brought in got a hundred. Andrew Symonds came in, smashed us everywhere. We couldn't bowl them out twice. It was the first of two complete whitewashes I've been on.

The problem you find yourselves in on tours like that is that you all know the questions, but no one really knows the answers. When Mitchell Johnson struck palpable fear into us seven years later, we all knew what he was going to do, we just didn't know how to deal with it. Speaking as a lower-order batsman, when the top order are coming back into the dressing room and saying, 'Literally no idea what to do here', it doesn't fill the place with optimism. It was the same in this series. We just didn't have the answers to McGrath, Warne et al. They would both retire, along with Damien Martyn and Justin Langer, after the series. They knew there'd be no better way to go out.

Not a great first Ashes for me, then.

The suits looked less smart on the flight home.

The Unlikely Lads

England vs Australia

12 July 2009

First Test, Day Five

Sophia Gardens, Cardiff

Match drawn

J M Anderson 21 not out

The anticipation for the 2009 Ashes was as high as anything I'd ever experienced as a player.

Even at the best of times during the build-up to an Ashes series, I find myself daily fielding the same dreaded question from a different stranger. I always know that it's reached fever pitch when the number of times it is asked is in double fingers every day. It was testament to what the 2005 Ashes had done for the game.

The return in England was multi-faceted in its meaning and narrative layers – for me personally, for the sides and for the thousands upon thousands from each country with an emotional investment. Kevin Pietersen had resigned from his captaincy in a public falling out with Peter Moores the year before and we'd been bowled out for

51 in West Indies that winter. The wheels were off. At the same time, Australia, still captained by Ricky Ponting, were desperate to exorcize the ghost of '05 and flew in, very understandably in the wake of the 2006 whitewash, as favourites. We were still some way away from the team-building exercises with special forces in Bavaria I described on page 136, but the Flower and Strauss regime had nonetheless begun to feed in its new measures and discipline. One thing we had drilled into us in some detail prior to the first test at Cardiff was the importance of seizing any kind of small initiative or edge.

We were looking for anything, any thread of hope we could grow throughout a series where the odds were stacked against us.

I don't think anyone, ourselves included, imagined that the moment in question would be provided by Monty Panesar and me … with the bat.

Exactly to the script, the Australians totally dominated the first four days of the test. We were left hanging on during the fifth day in the extremely unlikely hope of scraping a draw. A courageous effort, especially from Paul Collingwood, saw us reach the last hour with two wickets in tact. If I could hang in there with him, we might be OK. I was taking orders from him, just trying to do my bit.

On 74, he sliced a drive to cover. Caught. Out.

I remember watching his crushing disappointment, the body language of a man who had just batted heroically for nothing (it wouldn't have been the first time). More tellingly, it also betrayed that he had absolutely no confidence that Monty and I would survive the remaining 11.3 overs without losing our last wicket. As far as he was concerned, that was the test match over. To be fair, the sound of 16,000 people sighing simultaneously suggested he wasn't the only one.

I remember it now, Monty striding out.

I'd never seen anyone in the world with wider eyes.

He really didn't look as if he knew where he was.

He was in a total state of shock.

Despite being a huge talent of a spinner, if you need a gauge of Monty's ability, he was batting below me. For years I used to feel I had a sixth sense when a fielder was going to drop the ball off my bowling. Then I realized it was just whenever Monty was under it.

His batting was worse than his fielding.

That's about all you need to know.

No one gave us a hope in the world.

Suddenly, it struck me. *I* was the senior batsman here. This was the only opportunity I was ever going to get to farm the strike in a test match. I took to the role with some relish. It wasn't Colly giving the orders around here anymore. It was *me*. I'd seen enough of this kind of stuff at the other end to know what to do. I watched three balls whistle past my off stump. I looked around the field as if deliberating how I was going to get back on strike next over to protect Monty at the other end.

The responsibility.

What a buzz.

Peter Siddle was bowling extremely quickly. To this day, I don't think either Monty or I know what happened or how. It was a process. We'd survive an over, almost in dumbstruck awe of ourselves, and reconvene in the middle. I remember saying, 'Look, eventually we'll get out' and shrugging. He nodded. The old clock in the distance looked as if it was suspended. The hands just didn't seem to be moving. There was pressure, undoubtedly. From the middle, I could feel everyone's eyes focusing on every ball. The thing you find is, when you're out there, it's much easier. You're in control. Having watched the highlights some years later, though, I do have to say that I'm not sure anyone would opt for 'in control' as a neat summary of our last hour at the crease.

We survived two leg-before shouts. The odd one shot low across the surface just past my off stump.

We started to believe that we could make it to close of play.

The scrap, though admittedly heroic, was not without the odd comedic moment. Maybe becoming slightly over power hungry, I started desperately trying to get Monty off strike. The pitch was turning and Nathan Hauritz was bowling at Monty with the entire field surrounding the bat. He pushed the ball square and we manically set off for a run. With the benefit of hindsight, it might have been slightly ambitious. The Australians, if a bit stressed, were still annoyingly alert, and threw the ball at the non-striker's end.

Noticing how far out of his ground he was, Monty dived for the line.

It looked convincing enough at first from my end. If a little keen.

He dived way too early.

He landed flat on the pitch, stretched with his bat out, still short of his ground. He ended up like a beached salmon, leaping on his belly to try and remake his ground. He did. I'm not sure anyone in Cardiff knew how.

It was just about surviving any way we knew. We survived in some ways we didn't know.

Part of it lay in the art of eating up some time. Tying our shoelaces. Fixing our pads. Adjusting our helmet. It was weird, Monty and I just kept getting these little twinges that required urgent attention. Our physio at the time was an Australian, Steve McCague. His all-time hero was Ricky Ponting. As he ran onto the field in one of our 'emergency' call-outs, he went past said childhood hero. Ponting just turned to him and said, 'What the hell are you doing here, you fat ****?'

And they say never meet your heroes.

I tried to console him after the game that it had been a sensitive time to meet him.

Another problem was that one of the umpires, Aleem Dar, had quite limited English at the time. So on top of everything else there was genuine confusion in the middle as to how much time was left. No one seemed to know. We just kept shrugging and kept going. Walking as slowly as we could back to the crease between overs. The situation was made even more complex by the fact that we were close to the Australian score, albeit having batted an innings more. If we could get beyond parity, that would also eat some time into the day. I squeezed a couple through gully. Four runs. More time out of the game.

It was going to be our day.

Applause began to greet every ball survived. The whole flow of the game, and with it the series, had suddenly somehow swung wildly toward us in an hour of cricket. When the umpire eventually called time and the match a draw, Monty and I embraced briefly, but we hardly really celebrated. When teams save test matches like that you often see players running back into the dressing room or fist-pumping at everyone. We didn't do any of that. I think we were in a state of paralysed shock. I think everyone was. The place had erupted into a confused mixture of relief and euphoria. Cricket is a strange game like that. We had been absolutely beaten into the ground for pretty much five whole days and yet it was cause for celebration.

The Australians, having totally dominated and still being all square with four to play, were suddenly downbeat. I know from experience how draining it is to have not won a game you really should have. There's something humiliating about it, to have felt so close to the line and not been able to see it through. Suddenly you can *feel* all the effort, almost as if you physically become drained, and you have to drag yourself to the next game with the burden of it still weighing on you. Ricky Ponting, ever combative, spoke afterward to the cameras about having dominated the game and not being affected. The fact that we knew the Australian wives had ordered Champagne to the dressing room upon Monty's arrival at the crease, being so sure they were going to be celebrating imminently, suggested otherwise.

We liked the image of them sitting there, staring at bottles of unopened Champagne in the middle of the dressing room, just thinking, 'How?'

Monty wouldn't play a role again in the series. But in those 11.3 overs he might just have played the biggest one of anyone all summer. We retained the Ashes that year, winning the Oval decider to take the series 2-1.

All Your Christmases at Once

Australia vs England

26 December (Boxing Day) 2010

Fourth Test, Close of Day One

Melbourne Cricket Ground

Australia 98 all out

J M Anderson 16-4-44-4

England 151-0

While the 2010/11 Ashes tour is now painted forever in the mind as a once-in-a-lifetime, all-conquering performance over the Aussies, it's easy to forget that halfway through the series it was really in the balance. After three tests, going into Boxing Day at Melbourne, it was poised at 1-1. England had not come as close to anything like this in decades and we knew it. We'd taken the moral points in a draw at Brisbane, blunting the Australian attack's pride by ending up 517-1 while batting to 'save' the game, before winning by an innings in Adelaide and then being blown away by Mitchell Johnson, a fragment of a story to come, in Perth. Despite reaching Melbourne with honours even, we had undeniably disturbed an element of the Australian psyche and felt we had the upper hand. Much of the media didn't necessarily agree, though. Maybe I was just telling myself that to distract myself from my Christmas Day on the spare-parts table with Monty and Swanny the day before (*see* page 184).

The Boxing Day Test at the Melbourne Cricket Ground is, for most in Australia, the highlight of the sporting calendar. David Saker, our Australian bowling coach, would tell us with odd relish and twisted nostalgia how families celebrate Christmas, drink all day, then bounce out of bed the next morning at the prospect of berating some Poms. It's Pom-bashing day. Their favourite annual event. Given their success up until then (they had only been bowled out twice in that test three times in the previous 15 years), it was tantamount to watching *Home Alone* or *Elf* once a year. You knew how it ended. You knew you liked the ending. You repeated it every Christmas.

The MCG holds 96,000 people. (By way of comparison, Lord's holds 30,000 and Wembley 90,000 at most.) It's absolutely immense. One of the greatest sporting arenas in the entire world. Those 96,000 tickets, as they are every year without fail, were all sold. Every single seat. With everyone acutely aware of how much was at stake that morning, we could almost feel them baying for our blood. At the G, the dressing room is almost like it's in a dungeon. You enter the place underground and remain there until required. There is no view of the pitch. It really is akin to going into gladiatorial combat. You can almost feel the dust falling from the ceiling. You walk through the dark underbelly, your spikes echoing across the floor, while an intimidatingly faint sound, the unmistakable murmur of a lot of people anticipating a sporting slaughter, slowly becomes louder and louder as you move toward the light in the distance, gradually coming into focus.

It's like crossing into another dimension, from one world into the next.

The heat suddenly becomes intense and, as an England player, you are greeted, roundly and without exception, with deafening and distinctly aggressive boos. It's not any surprise that the Aussies have won so much there. It's genuinely intimidating. As far as cricketing experiences go, it really is like no other. We'd sat around on Christmas Day 24 hours earlier and many of the squad had divulged that they'd considered it a pinnacle of their career to be involved in a Boxing Day Test. I'm not sure many had dared dream of even winning until now. I'd sat there on my hands, keeping schtum, slightly concerned that the outcome of their dreams might not be what they had always wanted it to be. I'd experienced it before. Just being there, in your England whites, crossing through the dark underground into the piercing light as if you were being sent to your imminent death, was a thing.

We'd come too far, though, to just be part of the ceremony this time.

It was a tricky call before play because Straussy thought we should bat first. Andy Flower was convinced we should bowl. They rarely had such bi-polar opinions on something as vital as the toss on the first morning of a test. Dave Saker, the source of all knowledge when it came to matters with the ball, sided with Flower. He was adamant that batting would be a bad idea.

Straussy was probably the best captain I have ever played under.

He had the cricket brain, and the ability to deal with each player bespoke to their needs, as well as being able to lead from the front. Alongside that, while leaving you in no doubt of what he required from you, he had the good grace to listen to other opinions than his own. When we were run into the ground on the Bavaria trip, he was good at getting everyone to open up. We'd probably not been given the opportunity to be as honest as that until then. Once we had shared our fears for the tour, we found we all had the same doubts. Everyone was as vulnerable as everyone else. It made us all look out for each other a bit more. It was about trust and having the emotional dexterity to admit when you were wrong.

Straussy took heed of his own principles.

He listened to the advice. He trusted it.

He won the toss and bowled first.

I was glad to be getting into the game early. I felt I had the measure of some of their top order and I just wanted to be bowling. It didn't immediately go to plan. It felt tense. In my first spell, opening up against a backdrop of Aussies rubbing their hands together at having Englishmen on boundary ropes to shout at for an entire day, I was wicketless. It hadn't been chanceless, though. I tempted Shane Watson to drive at one outside off stump, which Colly, at full stretch to his left, spilled having done the hard work to get there. It was a tough one to get angry at, but also the kind of catch you'd usually expect him to take. It wasn't going to be one of those today, was it?

I began to fear the worst when KP then dropped a much simpler chance, again to Watson. These were the kind of chances you see on a highlights reel when they go through the key moments in a batsman's game-defining hundred. Your mind can do that after an incident like that. Then I had Phil Hughes caught behind, which on review was shown to have just clipped his shirt rather than anything else and was overturned.

Thankfully, we had a whole unit that had the bit between their teeth. Everyone was reaching a crescendo of sorts for that part of their career. Chris Tremlett, the real surprise package for the Aussies, was bowling fast, with steep bounce, and swinging it as well. It will have been a lot to deal with. They made it look that way, too; constantly hurried on shots and taking themselves for walks in between balls as if in the hope that when they returned to the crease some kind of curse would have been dispelled. Chris got Watson, then Ponting, while Bres – a surprise recall for the side, but an undefeated England test player at the time with the knack for rising to an occasion – got Phil Hughes.

We were into them. 37-3.

What happened next was, in all my Ashes experiences, one of the most unbelievable periods of play I've ever been involved in. I got Michael Hussey, edging behind to one that slanted across him. Mr Cricket, as they liked to call him, was a very big wicket at the time. He had single-handedly held the order up in previous tests and was the only player we were developing insecurities about being able to get out at all once he was in. My non-cricket tactic to him that tour was constantly calling him by his brother's name, Dave. Shot, Dave. Careful, Dave. Bit loose, Dave. I didn't relent. He would eventually snap during the Sydney test, barking back, 'It's Mike. Not Dave. MIKE.' That was as sure a sign as any that we were on top.

Anyway, back at Melbourne, at 58-4 we could suddenly sense a disconcerted collective gulping in the arena engulfing us, which itself was becoming less and less imposing in its stature. We had let Australia off the hook at 69-5 in Perth and were determined we weren't going to let that be the story of our series. Rain either side of lunch contributed to conditions that I knew would be helpful to me and I felt myself click into gear. One to Smith, again slanted across him. Nicked it. Gone. Same to Clarke. Nicked it. Gone. Mitchell Johnson. Leg cutter. Gone for 0. It was a delirious passage of play. I looked up as we were whooping and giggling with each other in the middle at the sight of Mitchell trudging off and the score was 77-8. 77-8!? Australia at the MCG on Boxing Day!? It was unheard of.

We bowled them out for 98.

They'd only been batting for just over three hours.

When Strauss and Cook were padding up, getting ready to go and bat – to their disbelief, only halfway through the second session – there was a strange sense of calm. We knew they'd bat through the rest of the day unharmed. And they did. It was a nice birthday present for Cooky. The ground, so swelling with vitriol and promise that morning, was nigh on empty by close, with only the English corner populated by the Barmy Army still present. I'm not one for records, really, but as they were read back to us at the press conference it was hard to keep a hint of a smile at bay. The lowest first-innings total ever at the MCG. The lowest Australian total against England at home since 1936. The lowest score in Australia since 1984. There had been one day of cricket and we'd won the test already.

Psychologically, that was probably the moment when we won the Ashes, too. We went on to take the series 3-1. It had taken 24 years for a touring England side to do that. None of my heroes growing up had managed it.

It really was a very special day. The most surreal of my entire playing career.

Worth a Review After All

England vs Australia

14 July 2013

First Test, Day Five

Trent Bridge, Nottingham

England won by 14 runs

J M Anderson Man of the Match

24-2-85-5

31.5-11-73-5

Four years after Monty's and my left-field headline grabbing in the opening act of '09, we'd hung on to the Ashes for consecutive series. This time the Australians, now under the leadership of Michael Clarke, came as underdogs, having been beaten in Australia in the even-by-now-infamous '10/11 tour. With their tails up and pride dented, we knew how significant the opening exchanges would be. With many five-test series, though this is obviously not totally definitive, the first match tends to set the tone for the remainder of the summer. Both sides are like cowboys in a western, sizing each other up, preparing to draw first.

From the outside, this one at Trent Bridge, I am told, had just the same amount of unbearable tension as Cardiff four years before. I found myself in the centre of it again. This time – and, in all honesty, despite the novel rush of batting with sudden responsibility – I was far more comfortable that my role was with the ball.

Like a story being retold, but with plot twists decorated throughout, this one felt like being inside Edgbaston '05 at times. As I've mentioned before, it was easier actually being involved. Control is the key. When you're a fan, or a player watching from the dressing room, the helplessness is the thing that plays games with you. I could barely watch that test. England won by two runs. In many people's eyes, it was the greatest test of all time.

This one came close.

It was a bit of an odd-ball five days.

Michael Clarke was the man to target in their side. I knew the exact corridor I needed to bowl to him. There was an absolutely minute window that would be the difference between him driving you, guiding you through the leg side or genuinely playing and missing.

It's one of the most perfect balls I've ever bowled.

It pitched on off stump, moved away a fraction and clipped the stump.

I thought it had gone past everything.

Then I heard the noise.

The most perfect noise that a swing bowler who prides himself on precision and execution can hear. It was not dramatic, stumps cartwheeling or multiple crashes. It was the tiniest 'clink'. The kind of sound that the untrained ear would dismiss as nothing. But to those attuned, it was unmistakably the bail at the top of off stump being dislodged at speed.

There are all sorts of premeditated celebrations these days. Our one-day side in the West Indies in early 2019 had to get very used to watching Sheldon Cotterell's salute celebration. It takes quite a long time to execute. His team-mates have to wait next to him while he completes it. I've never been one for any of that. I feel it would be tempting fate to have a celebration planned. I just let my instinct decide how I'm going to respond. Back in 2013 I was always reminded of the time when the camera caught Mitchell Johnson, at the non-striker's end, saying, 'Why you chirping now, you're not getting any wickets?', before I ran in and bowled Ryan Harris. It was one of those unrepeatable moments where everything synchronizes and happens to be caught perfectly on camera. I couldn't resist turning to Mitchell and putting my finger to my lips. But there have been a few moments where I've looked back and thought, 'What was I doing?!', too, like the unpremeditated windmill I did when I bowled Mohammed Yousef years ago.

With the bowling itself, though, I love it when a plan comes off.

It came off to Clarke. It was the kind of ball you needed to bowl to him early, before he got set, otherwise he could do some serious damage. It sparked a celebration where I was screaming, both hands pointing at the stumps. It's the only time I've done that. He probably didn't need to be told. He was already walking off.

During that first innings, we had the Australians in real trouble at 117-9 when a 19-year-old called Ashton Agar came to the crease. We knew very little about him. He'd been drafted in last minute, his family flown over from Melbourne, to breathe some new energy into their side. A man after my own heart as a number 11, he put my own antics in perspective with a counter-punching 98 from 101 balls on debut. The highest score by a number 11 in test history. It was a very rare innings. To be honest, I think the Australians were as surprised as we were.

It's the first time I've ever played against a specialist number 11.

It was a knock so full of youthful ignorance and exuberance that when he fell just short of a century, middling a short ball straight to Swanny at deep mid-wicket, the whole ground fleetingly forgot about the rivalry and rose to their feet as he smiled and shrugged his way off.

The game had swung back and forth in an uncharacteristically unpredictable and chaotic way for a couple of days when we arrived for the fifth day with Australia requiring 137 runs with four wickets remaining.

It couldn't have been tighter.

The main source of concern for us was that their wicketkeeper, Brad Haddin, was still at the crease. Haddin was a seriously competitive man, always talking behind the stumps, the engine room of the unit if you like, with whom we had built up a back story of posturing since 2010/11. In fact, we inadvertently had him to thank for one of the moments that had triggered a collective belief in ourselves that winter. Every time Steve Finn – who was 21 and playing against the Aussies for the first time – walked past him in the first test, Haddin, possibly having identified him as a player who could be confronted without challenge, would sledge him. At tea, Finny came in a little exasperated and said, 'It's getting to me a bit. Every time I walk past him, he's saying something to me.' Our response was, straight after the break, to go right up to Haddin on the field, in a pack, and say to him, 'Why are you picking on the younger guy? We're all here if you've got something to say.' He backed off. That's when we knew that we had them. It fell together after that.

But here he was again. Cricket has a habit of allowing people to set some stories straight. The worry was that he was going to do it here. It was an odd wicket for English conditions, slow and low, reversing a little, the kind of track that you can find yourself ineffectual on if you don't have patience and a few tricks. It was about persistence and, like anything, luck.

It was probably exactly the right moment in my career to find myself in that situation.

The problem was, Alastair Cook identified that too. He gave me the ball and he wouldn't take it off me. I bowled for 13 overs in the morning. Thanks, mate. The adrenaline of the situation kept me going. The throbbing of the crowd around us, intensifying in volume as we got deeper into the game, until suddenly, a disturbed hush, everyone too involved to dare move. I felt in a really good rhythm, as if my action was naturally taking care of me, and I let it be my guide. I just kept going. I would have gone on forever, until I dropped or someone said stop.

We had a little period into the day when it suddenly didn't feel as if it was going to happen. Ashton Agar, promoted to 8, batted for two hours with Haddin and they were crawling toward the target. There were a few misfields off my bowling and I don't think you'd have needed to be a mystic to read my thoughts. I might have let my body language show some feelings. Broady probably mentioned it (in fact I know he did – *see* page 203). I won't contest it. He was right. I was wound up. Red mist is absolutely a thing for a fast bowler.

I was mid-red mist.

When we reached the tea break, they needed 20 runs with one wicket in hand. Haddin, with ample assistance from James Pattinson, had started to take the game away from us. I had become very tense. They would have won the game if there'd been half an hour more uninterrupted play. It was a blessing. Breaks almost always suit the fielding side, because a batsman needs to get set again. There's a fresh opportunity.

Finally. I've found something that bowlers have in their favour in this godforsaken game.

When we got into the dressing room, there was a surprising atmosphere of calm and focus. Thinking back on it makes me really appreciate what a special side that was. We didn't panic. We always knew that we could find something to get us out of any situation. We had an inner belief in ourselves that had taken four years to establish. I had an opportunity both to apologize and to thank Stuart for setting me straight on the field and, as I collected my thoughts, Cooky came and sat next to me to tell me I was bowling straight after tea. I'd gathered as much. Matt Prior, vice-captain at the time, said a few words, reminding us that all the pressure was on them. We walked out in a different state of clarity.

Haddin chipped away at a few.

I bowled him one slightly wider than I had before. He flayed a bit at it, missed it and it sailed through to Matt behind the stumps. At least, I thought he missed it. Matt and the slips jumped up and, hedging my bets, I went up with them too, if not in entirely convincing fashion. It's always worth asking. Haddin was already preparing for his next ball.

Not out.

Agreed.

I was about to walk back to my mark when, to my surprise, I saw Cooky signalling for a review with an uncharacteristic degree of certainty. As we got together to discuss it, I didn't want to break it to the others that their wishfulness was clouding their judgement. I thought they'd all been spending too much time with Stuart Broad. Literally everything is out when he is bowling. It's not gamesmanship, either. He genuinely thinks everything is out. He'd review every ball he bowled to the third umpire if he could. Anyway, as we were congregated, stood waiting, we asked Haddin.

He just replied, as if reluctantly relinquishing a secret that he knew was going to cause pandemonium, 'Yeah. I think I've hit it.'

(Quite often you'll ask the batsman if they've hit the ball. They always say they know whether or not they've hit it. And they usually say they haven't.)

What?

Yeah, I've hit it.

Simultaneously, the big screen showed hot spot, the faintest of inside edges.

It's out.

We've won.

That was it. The whole of Trent Bridge lost the plot. There's a great photo of it somewhere: the whole team setting off in different directions in a moment of wild jubilation. One thing that technology has been great for is that, in the moment of winning the game, the team can be huddled together, awaiting a decision. So, when it comes up on the big screen, the response is like a new year's celebration meets winning the World Cup.

I was so sure that I was all right running in all day. It didn't even hurt. The fact that I collapsed and fell asleep in the dressing room suggests it might have taken more out of me than I was prepared to admit.

We won that series 3-0. It was the last great collective statement from that side.

And so it goes on. There have been many Ashes moments since. Of the last four series, there's been a bit of snatching back and forth by whoever is at home. After our famous side full of disparate and dedicated individuals had achieved that notable success of beating them 3-0 in England in 2013, we were blown away by Mitchell Johnson in the immediate return series. We then upset the odds to take the urn back in 2015, winning the series 3-2, a personal highlight being taking 6-47 at Edgbaston to put us 2-1 up, before being dragged around Australia in an all-too-familiar-of-late drubbing down under in 2017/18.

Still, I've had far more success than many of my heroes, having won the Ashes four times. It's caused my body quite a lot of torment. And all for what? A tiny little urn supposedly containing the ashes of a bail burned in 1882 to signify the death of English cricket. It can feel slightly Pythonesque when you compete for months in unrelenting intensity and for your troubles are handed a trophy roughly the size of a pencil sharpener when you win.

It does tend to be moving for players, though. I remember Swanny getting his hand on the Ashes for the first time. He was overcome with emotion, like reaching the promised land or pulling the sword from the stone. A single tear on the precipice of falling from his cheek, he lifted the urn into the air when he noticed an inscription on the bottom. As if he was Indiana Jones transcribing an ancient tapestry, he carefully brought it back to eye level. £4.95. Lord's shop. 'Oh, for...'

CHAPTER 8

And Another Thing...

I constantly, to this day, misread

whether it's one or two kisses

The Curious Case of Test Cricket

If the question I've had to field the most across my career is 'Are we gonna to win the Ashes, then?', it is very closely followed by:

'Is test cricket dying?'

Test cricket, you'd be led to believe, has been in serious threat of extinction ever since its inception. People are absolutely obsessed with the notion of it surviving or otherwise. If I'm asked about saving it, I'm never sure what to say. Save it from what? Is it being attacked? Has it asked for our help? It's hard to have an answer. The best response I've heard yet is from David Lloyd. He was asked and simply replied, 'Test cricket has been dying for 57 years.' I always feel the question is misplaced if it's asked of someone like me. I've been playing test cricket for a decade and a half. I'm the last person with any answers. I do often wonder what reaction people are searching for: do they think I'll point my head to the sky, muse and say, 'Life finds a way'?

It's as if some people want to preserve an idea of test cricket in formaldehyde, ensuring it both never changes and never decays, parallel *to* but not a part *of* a world that is continually demanding evolution. The modern worry is that the invasion of shorter and shorter forms of the game nullifies the stock of the purest form. T20 cricket has become a phenomenon, attracting huge crowds and luring young players to play for franchises all over the world, making more than twice the money for less than half the work. I don't blame anyone for that. But many 'traditionalists' see this as a direct threat to test cricket. Everyone, it seems, has their own bespoke concern for it and, with that, an opinion on how to save it, too.

To be fair, I do understand why. Test cricket *is* a rare thing, courageously long in a world of clickbait and short attention spans. But, ironically, therein lies both its charm and the key to its survival. It's not like everything else. There is nothing in the world close to it.

There are two very common criticisms:

IT'S BORING. NOTHING SEEMS TO BE HAPPENING

Trust me. I've had my moments myself. Meandering phases of play, standing in the field for two days, working like a dog. There are times I'd wholeheartedly agree. It can be a right pain. What time teaches, though, is that it's all in the suffering and the patience. If you read a good book, or watch a really great film, there will doubtlessly be moments when it *seems* as if there's not much going on. You forgive and endure the supposed lull because you trust that there is a purpose to it and a narrative arc. When you reach the end, the bit that felt pointless suddenly becomes the most important part of the whole thing. In hindsight, it has tension and layers that act as the foundation for everything that happened after. Now, I'm not encouraging the idea of more test cricket with *even less* happening;

what I am saying is, it's part of the experience, and those changes of pace are what make it the never-ending drama it is.

HOW CAN SOMETHING THAT LASTS FIVE DAYS END IN A DRAW WHEN T20 GIVES YOU A RESULT IN A FEW HOURS?

It's mostly Americans who ask that one. Try to look at it this way.

Cricket is *Revolver* by the Beatles. T20 is 'Yellow Submarine'. Test cricket is 'Tomorrow Never Knows'.

They both belong on the same album. 'Yellow Submarine' is great. It's catchy and instantly recognizable. Everyone knows 'Yellow Submarine'. It doesn't matter what age you are, you get it. However, if you listen to it ten times in a row, you'll be so saccharined up to the eyeballs that you'll be cross-eyed. You would be forgiven for wondering, 'There must be more to the Beatles than this.' T20 is the same. It has action, there are fireworks, it's over quickly. You watch it and think, 'Oh, I get it.' It is, if you will, a gateway drug.

'Tomorrow Never Knows' is tricky at first, irregular and at odds with the other song structures on *Revolver*. It has rules and laws all of its own. Its genius is that as you live with it, you keep finding new things. There are layers on it that make it last forever. Its innovation is built into its DNA. Whatever has happened since in music, it still feels brand new. It's test cricket. It survives. The band is the same. The instruments are the same. The album is the same. The music is very different.

Still with me?

Test cricket is a roast. T20 is an ice cream.

Ice cream is great. You eat it quickly. It's a rush. An ice cream is an ice cream. Nobody dislikes ice cream. But if you try to eat a diet solely of ice cream, you are going to become aware of its limitations very quickly.

A roast has *dimensions*. It gives you all the nourishment you need. You eat it slowly, appreciating the effort that has gone into making it. You look forward to roasts for a whole week. It has enough in it for everyone to find their own joy in there. Sometimes, a roast won't get it right. There's no gravy. The Yorkshires are missing. The potatoes are burned. It makes you wonder why you bother with roasts and why you wasted your time dreaming of it all week. When you get the right one, though, there's nothing better in the whole world.

Hope that helps.

One thing that seems pertinent to me in making the case for test cricket, despite the odds and slightly improbable lifespan, is that you tend to forever remember test matches that happened decades ago. The smallest details. They somehow embed themselves as stories inside your skull. Somehow, for some reason, they feel meaningful. Maybe it's because a test goes on for so long that it really does allow the fan to take every kind of metaphorical journey inside it. All of life is in there. The bare-bones reality. With T20 cricket, despite it being dramatic and exciting and absolutely worth its footing in the world, the majority of games do tend to disappear from memory almost instantly. I played 20 T20s for England. I don't remember any of them. That could just be me, though.

It's about what you put your currency in. The money being paid to players to play franchise cricket is ridiculous these days. I understand why anyone would focus purely on it. Our careers are short, after all. But the real meaning comes from looking at someone like Virat Kohli. He's a master of all forms of the game. He could easily go around the world making multi-millions playing T20 and appearing for India in short-form cricket. He chooses to minimize that so that he can captain India in test cricket. That's where his priority lies. He knows that it is the peak of the sport and, in creating a legacy, the only place he will truly be remembered. I've got to admit I didn't think so favourably about this in the summer of 2018 when I was locked in a constant duel with him. I didn't get him out.

The same goes for some of our current batting line-up: Joe Root, Jos Buttler, Ben Stokes, Moeen Ali and so on. They are capable of playing any form of the game at the highest level. They could take their pick. They choose to prioritize test cricket because they understand it's where the substantial measure of themselves will be made. Along with it, though, they bring a whole other dimension to the game. A new generation's take on an old classic. The shots they are capable of are absolutely jaw-dropping. Some of their repertoire didn't even exist ten years ago. I spend net sessions scratching my head at some of the things they do. They've learned those skills in T20 and brought them into test cricket, slowly forming a fascinating hybrid.

If you speak to any of the great batsmen with those skills, they will tell you that the real art is when those dynamic cricketers can walk into a test match and learn to bat without constantly going up through the gears. You rarely have to think about anything else in short form than smash, smash, smash. The demands of test cricket mean you need to accelerate, bat naturally; then the situation might require you to go into your shell for a moment, survive, then accelerate again. It's this intelligence and foresight that makes it a form beyond all others in the game. Like anything, it needs idols to keep regenerating the next batch of torch-bearers. So long as the aforementioned as well as some other names across the world – Steve Smith of Australia, Kane Williamson of New Zealand, Jason Holder of West Indies – continue to recognize that, the game will survive.

Certainly for a bowler, the disparity between the skills required in test cricket and in its shorter-form siblings is becoming wider all the time. Whereas I've learned my craft as a student of the long form, being able to bowl exactly where I want to with a plan, short-form bowling is wildly diverse. Bowlers need huge variations. It's all about the total element of surprise for the batsmen, who are trying to cart everything out of the ground with far less comparative risk or value on their wicket. There are some extremely highly skilled bowlers learning to survive from getting slapped everywhere with admirable dexterity. The problem is, though, this mixed-bag approach is often rewarded to the point where you're not sure even the bowler knows what's going to come out. If the bowler doesn't, even less chance the batsman does. That's where there may be a slight issue developing in breeding fast bowlers for tests with the same ability to keep the game at the standard it's been at historically. When the short-form bowlers have success and are 'promoted', they can occasionally lack the discipline that was drilled into previous generations when a batsman really puts a value on their wicket. The question these days for those hardy souls making it through the ranks as fast bowlers is: do you want to a) suffer for your art in the longest form, toiling around the county circuit in front of handfuls of people in a bid to become a specialist in your craft or b) get carted around stadiums all over the world for good money? You can't hold it against those who choose the second, but I hope there continue to be enough who decide on the first.

It's a life of thankless rejection either way, after all.

Don't get me wrong. I love watching T20. I'm often glad I don't have to play in it anymore. I'd get neck damage watching my deliveries sail out of grounds all over the world. It's become the bowler's lot. That's the worry for me. It needs to be more of a duel than a bowler teeing the ball up for batsmen to hit it out the ground. That will only last so long on a superficial level. Cricket is such a special game for allowing every single type of person to live within it: the slightly overweight crafty spinner, the athletic fast bowler, the thinker and tactician, the motor-mouth wicketkeeper. As soon as it becomes a one-sided slug fest, the danger is that it will lose one of its most vital and central aspects.

I'm behind the small changes that have been happening to the game of late. I think it needs to keep adapting. The numbers on the back of shirts in tests recently introduced seems like a common-sense measure to help people who are new to cricket to identify the players on the pitch. There can't be much wrong with that. I didn't really understand the commotion about it or the arguments that say it will take away from tradition. Little things like that, which help without detracting from the game itself, can't hurt. But what about sponsors on the shirts? Do we want to go back to playing in Dennis Lillee's work shirts? Would that be better? To dress pretending it's still the 1970s?

Test cricket's Achilles heel can be its weakness for nostalgia. We're all guilty of it. You remember how it resonated with you when you were young and can become desperate for the same feeling to be passed on. It's all in your mind's eye. I will always remember the cricket of the mid-1990s through a romanticized lens. Donald to Atherton. Curtly and Courtney. It was available to me through terrestrial television and, because of my dad and my local club, I dived in. People older than me will point to Botham's Ashes in 1981, younger to Freddie's in 2005. They were all portals into the game, making it widely accessible and then backed up by knowing somewhere you could go and play. The most important part is that cricket is still able to reach people in that way. The game will do the rest. Some will fall in love. Some will not. Test cricket is like a good piece of art – it might divide opinion but will continue to last, as long as it is not hidden away in some over-protected corner talking to itself. It tends to come up with its own answers. The last couple of years have produced some of the most memorable test matches of all time.

In honesty, I think cricket, in general, is as strong as it's ever been. It's really in a great position. There are some amazing T20 competitions across the world if you like the white-ball stuff. If you want test cricket, there's loads of that, too. What's not to love?

The Complications of Being
a Shy Fast Bowler

I've got used to being two totally different people.

It's been a constant contradiction across my life that, off a cricket field, I'm a very shy person and on it I sometimes terrify even myself. I think it throws people quite often. Outside the cricketing world, I am intensely socially awkward. I'm always the one who will go to shake someone's hand, miss it and shake them on the wrist, or misread the vital decision on whether to touch fists or high-five and end up holding someone's clenched fist, shaking it up and down. It's happened more than I dare mention. I constantly, to this day, misread whether it's one or two kisses. I'm still unsure which is the right one in which situation. I'll leave the poor woman I'm introduced to hanging, realize too late that a second kiss on the other cheek was required and then go and kiss them on the nose as they've decided to turn away.

It doesn't make any difference how many wickets you take. It doesn't matter if you've taken Sachin Tendulkar's wicket more than anyone in the history of test cricket. The whole stand named after you at Old Trafford will not step in to save you. None of it solves the daily conundrum of small talk and the treacherous first meets. It's strange because there probably was a time when I imagined that it might. I've made peace with it now. When I go to a party or some kind of social gathering, I'll steel myself to expect that I will leave with my brain saying to my mouth, 'What was that crap? You embarrassed me in there.' I've reached acceptance. Sometimes, even, it reassures me. It's confirmation that I'm still sane, that those small things are still as earth-shatteringly uncomfortable to me as they've always been.

On my second or third date with Daniella, we were sitting in a pub in Maida Vale. I thought it was going relatively well. An hour into the admittedly stunted conversation, she snapped and looked at me square in the eye:

'Look, you're going to have to speak. Otherwise I'm going to leave. Just give me *something* here.'

Almost beyond my conscious grasp, I'd hardly said a word. It's something over the course of a career and an adulthood that I've learned to gently tease out of myself. Just finding a way of day-to-day simple functioning in the 'real world'. My first year in the England team I barely spoke either. I spent a year in the corner, watching how it all worked and trying to stay out of the way until I was asked to bowl. I must have grown comfortable relatively sharpish, because a year into my career I found myself in the dressing room taking the piss out of my captain, Nasser. He turned to me and said, 'I preferred when you were a mute.' I guess he and Daniella were after different kinds of relationships.

It's been the same with my work with the media, my comfort in front of a camera or microphone. To begin with, I would be interviewed on television and find myself totally seizing up. One-word answers were a stretch. It's something I've had to really slowly talk myself round and into. I still get it now with commentating; I'll be thinking, 'What's that word that I need, help!' inside my head. The odd thing, though, is I've surprised myself in that I really enjoy it. It's come with a decade and a half of slowly building a bank of confidence that I deserve to be there and, in turn, that I will have something productive to say about the game. I like presenting and being in front of the camera. Maybe because it's been such a battle to get used to it, the fact that I am beginning to develop skills at something that, unlike bowling, didn't come naturally to me at all, is rewarding in its own way.

I don't want to make this sound like the scene in *Wayne's World*, where they go back stage to meet Alice Cooper and are mortified to find him to be nothing like what they imagined but, off a cricket pitch, I absolutely hate confrontation, too. I will do whatever I can to avoid one-on-one confrontation with anyone.

I'm not sure what happens to me when I get on a cricket pitch.

The first time I really shocked myself with the difference was during a county game. I was really good friends with Vikram Solanki. He was playing for Worcestershire at the time and we'd spent a lot of the season together playing for England. The club was having a benefit year and he asked me to write in the brochure. Later that season, Lancashire played Worcestershire at Old Trafford. I was bowling like rubbish. Vikram was smashing me everywhere. The red mist came down. I just lost the plot. I really went hard at him. Pretty personal too. 'I just can't stand you. You're all nicey-nice off the field but deep down you're a pr***.' It was as if I wasn't in control of the things I was saying. After the day's play, I came off the field and went to my spot in the dressing room. There was his brochure with a Post-it note: 'To Jimmy. Thanks for your kind words. Love Vikram.'

Occasionally I have empathy for the Incredible Hulk. I think all us fast bowlers do. We're driven to madness. When the Hulk comes back round and can't remember what he's just done or the reasons for it. That rings a bell. People tell me what I've done and I have no recollection of it whatsoever. I have definitely had moments of coming to in the dressing room and thinking, 'Who was that who was just shouting like that?' I'll be asking myself inside my head, 'What the hell are you doing? Who is that idiot!?' In any other situation than a cricket pitch, I'd be mortified at myself for acting like that. I wouldn't dare. I still come up against people who are completely shocked when I spray them on the field. And those who are completely shocked when I don't off it. Your perception of me will probably ultimately hinge on whether or not you've played cricket against me. If I've bowled at you, it's likely to not be particularly positive.

The switch between the two personalities has never been conscious. The difference between them has always been quite natural. The competitive inertia has meant that suddenly, when involved in a cricket match, I will be engaged in a different way. I know that a lot of cricketers do have an issue with blending what is required from them on the field and how it affects their life off it. Mark Butcher, for example, has spoken to me about how he was actually relieved when he eventually retired because he had felt survival at test level required him to invent a personality. He decided he needed to be ruthless on a level that wasn't natural to him, so had to force himself to become more selfish and robust than he would otherwise have been. In time, he struggled to separate that on-field personality (a method that was successful) with his off-field one (a person he was beginning to dislike).

I've been lucky in that way, in that I've taken to the demands of the highest level quite naturally. It has given me real purpose in my life without making me feel I need to alter my personality off the pitch. The troubles arise when people have projected ideas about who you are that you are never quite sure that you can match. It leaves you in a bit of a no-man's-land with what's expected of you.

The thing I'd worry about most was becoming the shy person on the field. I'll probably know that my cricket days are gone when my off-field self begins finding himself on the pitch. I think what I've been good at, ruthless as it may sound, is being able to turn off from any outside influences, friends and family or anything else, as soon as I go to play cricket. It requires complete focus. When I play, I have always been able to shut whatever is happening in 'real life' out immediately. I'm lucky in that regard because it's an area where many of us have struggled. I couldn't have reached that place without Daniella. The effort and tunnel vision required to play the game, plus being away all the time, were a shock to her at first. But she's been amazing ever since she got her head around it. She lets me get on with it, understands what it requires and gets on with her life separately. We both know that the other is there if we need them to be, but the balancing act of a relationship alongside the intensity of my work is something you need to be lucky with and find a patient and like-minded person.

I know I've spent the entirety of this book moaning about cricket. But deep down, I'm very grateful for it. It picked me up in Burnley and has taken me around the world on ever-increasing adventures. It's widened my horizons beyond what any words could describe. It's been a community, firstly an imaginary one through the television, then a real one in Burnley and eventually a worldwide one. I didn't think I'd end up as the highest fast-bowling wicket-taker in the history of the game. I was only after a Peugeot with my name on it.

It's like anything. You need to work at it. It's all a constant work in progress.

Genius is in the act of showing up.

Bowl. Sleep. Repeat.

Jimmy's Greatest Hits

The Best of (as of beginning of 2019)...

5 TEST INNINGS AT HOME

20.1-5-42-7
England vs West Indies, Lord's, 7–9 September 2017

21.3-8-43-7
England vs New Zealand, Trent Bridge, 5–8 June 2008

15-8-17-6
England vs Pakistan, Trent Bridge, 29 July–1 August 2010

14.4-2-47-6
England vs Australia, Edgbaston, 29–31 July 2015

11.4-6-16-5
England vs Sri Lanka, Headingley, 19–21 May 2016

5 TEST INNINGS OVERSEAS

12.4-5-42-6
England vs West Indies, Kensington Oval, 1–3 May 2015

22-7-5-43-5
England vs Australia, Adelaide Oval, 2–6 December 2017

30-13-46-5
England vs West Indies, Kensington Oval, 23–26 January 2019

21.1-2-63-5
England vs South Africa, Newlands, 3–7 January 2010

20.3-5-72-5
England vs Sri Lanka, Galle International Stadium, 26–29 March 2012

5 TEST MATCHES AT HOME

37-15-11-71
England vs Pakistan, Trent Bridge, 29 July–1 August 2010

25.1-11-45-10
England vs Sri Lanka, Headingley 19–21 May 2016

55.5-13-158-10
England vs Australia, Trent Bridge, 10–14 July 2013

25.2-10-43-9
England vs India, Lord's, 9–12 August 2018

36.1-12-73-9
England vs West Indies, Lord's, 7–9 September 2017

5 TEST MATCHES OVERSEAS

43.3-2-161-8
England vs South Africa, Newlands, 3–7 January 2010

25.4-9-77-7
England vs West Indies, Kensington Oval, 1–3 May 2015

48.1-12-127-7
England vs Australia, Sydney Cricket Ground, 3–7 January 2011

35-6-130-7
England vs New Zealand, Basin Reserve, 13–17 March 2008

41.1-15-69-6
England vs Pakistan, Sharjah, 1–5 November 2015

ONE INNINGS OF NOTE WITH THE BAT

81, England vs India, Trent Bridge, 29 July 2014

5 BEST ODI PERFORMANCES AT HOME

10-2-23-4
England vs India, The Rose Bowl, 21 August 2007

5-0-4-18
England vs Sri Lanka, The Oval, 28 June 2011

30-13-46-5
England vs West Indies, Kensington Oval, 23–26 January 2019

21.1-2-63-5
England vs South Africa, Newlands, 3–7 January 2010

20.3-5-72-5
England vs Sri Lanka, Galle International Stadium, 26–29 March 2012

5 TEST MATCHES AT HOME

37-15-71-11
England vs Pakistan, Trent Bridge, 29 July–1 August 2010

25.1-11-45-10
England vs Sri Lanka, Headingley 19–21 May 2016

55.5-13-158-10
England vs Australia, Trent Bridge, 10–14 July 2013

25.2-10-43-9
England vs India, Lord's, 9–12 August 2018

36.1-12-73-9
England vs West Indies, Lord's, 7–9 September 2017

5 TEST MATCHES OVERSEAS

43.3-2-161-8
England vs South Africa, Newlands, 3–7 January 2010

25.4-9-77-7
England vs West Indies, Kensington Oval, 1–3 May 2015

48.1-12-127-7
England vs Australia, Sydney Cricket Ground, 3–7 January 2011

35-6-130-7
England vs New Zealand, Basin Reserve, 13–17 March 2008

41.1-15-69-6
England vs Pakistan, Sharjah, 1–5 November 2015

ONE INNINGS OF NOTE WITH THE BAT

81, England vs India, Trent Bridge, 29 July 2014

5 BEST ODI PERFORMANCES AT HOME

10-2-23-4
England vs India, The Rose Bowl, 21 August 2007

5-0-4-18
England vs Sri Lanka, The Oval, 28 June 2011

9-2-27-4

England vs Pakistan, The Oval, 20 June 2003

9.4-0-44-4

England vs South Africa, The Oval, 31 August 2012

10-0-55-4

England vs Australia, Trent Bridge, 17 September 2009

5 BEST ODI PERFORMANCES OVERSEAS

10-3-23-5

England vs South Africa, St George's Park, 29 November 2009

9.5-2-34-5

England vs New Zealand, McLean Park, 20 February 2013

8.3-2-18-4

England vs India, Brisbane Cricket Ground, 20 January 2015

10-1-25-4

England vs Netherlands, Buffalo Park, 16 February 2003

10-2-29-4

England vs Pakistan, Newlands, 22nd February 2003

THE NUMBERS AS THEY STAND

Test matches: 151
Wickets: 584
Average: 26.83

ODIs: 194
Wickets: 269
Average: 29.22

First Class: 248
Wickets: 959
Average: 24.92

Highest wicket-taking fast bowler in test history

Highest English wicket-taker of all time

REST OF THE WORLD ODI XI

V Sehwag

A C Gilchrist

B McCullum

V Kohli

Y Singh

M S Dhoni (captain and wicketkeeper)

J D P Oram

B Lee

S E Bond

S Akhtar

12th man: M G Bevan

COUNTY TEAM-MATES XI

S M Katich (captain)

K K Jennings

S G Law

C L Hooper

N H Fairbrother

A Symonds

W K Hegg (wicketkeeper)

G Chapple

P J Martin

M Muralitharan

G Keedy

12th man: K W Hogg

Index

Picture Credits

i © Burnley Express; *ii* Michael Steele/Allsport/Getty Images; *iii* Tom Shaw/Getty Images; *iv* & *v* Stuart Forster/Getty Images; *vi* Adam Pretty/Getty Images; *vii* Tommy Hindley/Getty Images; *viii* Philip Brown/Getty Images; *ix*, *xii*, *xiv* Gareth Copley/Getty Images; *xi* Andrew Fosker/Seconds Left/Shutterstock; *xiii* Matthew Impey/Shutterstock; *xv* Glyn Kirk/AFP/Getty Images; *xvi* Mark Kerton/Action Plus via Getty Images; *xvii* Andrew Fosker/Bpi/Shutterstock; *xviii* Philip Brown/Getty Images; *xix* Philip Brown

Acknowledgements

It's been a huge pleasure writing *Bowl. Sleep. Repeat* and there are many people to thank for it finding its way into your hands now. Firstly, I'd like to thank Felix for all the time spent putting this together. We collated this during the away test series in Sri Lanka and the West Indies, as well as stolen moments before and after recording our weekly BBC podcast *Tailenders*. We wanted to pack in as much as possible on the truths of what playing for England is like. I think we managed it. Sincere thanks to Trevor Davies and all at Octopus publishing for taking the leap of faith in putting it together and for their constant engagement and support in the project. Their editorial team of Polly Poulter and Caroline Taggart have been a joy to work with. Special mention to my management; Nicola Wright and all at M & C Saatchi for their ongoing oversight, dedication and not least helping me to find time to fit the process in between England tours. A massive thank you also to Nick Walters, David Luxton and all at DLA Associates for sowing the seeds of the idea, facilitating the collaboration with Felix and being on-hand constantly since to help this book become a reality. Of course, I'd also like to extend huge thanks to my main two bowling partners over the years, Broady and Swanny, for their contributions and willingness to be involved. To that end, thanks to the ECB, too, for their support of this project and over the years. Lastly, Felix and I would both like to send the biggest Go Well of all time to Greg James, Mark 'Sharky' Sharman and Mattchin Tendulkar for providing the highlight to almost every week for the last couple of years on *Tailenders*. #Tailendersoftheworlduniteandtakeover